Praise for Brian Leaf's *Top 50 Skills* Series

Top 50 Skills for a Top Score: SAT Math

"What a surprise, what a relief! An SAT guide that actually meets you where you are, talks to you with wit and compassion, and clears away the panic of test-taking. And, the writing is first-rate too. Bravo Brian Leaf."

Rebecca Pepper Sinkler, former Editor, *The New York Times Book Review*

"I enjoyed the informal writing style, and the flash cards for math are brilliant! Students are used to stacks of vocabulary words in preparation for the verbal portion of the test, why not drills on flash cards for the math section?"

Denise Brown-Allen, Ed.D., Upper School Director, The Pingry School

"If everyone starts using Brian's secrets and strategies, The College Board and ETS are going to have to rewrite the SAT!!"

Max Shelton, George Washington University, Class of 2012

Top 50 Skills for a Top Score: SAT Critical Reading and Writing

"Brian Leaf has hacked off the head of America's high school boogie man—the dreaded SAT. He clearly lays out how the test works, accessible preparation strategies, and how to maximize one's score. Any college applicant can benefit from his thoughtful and well-researched advice."

Joie Jager-Hyman, former Assistant Director of Admissions, Dartmouth College, author of *Fat Envelope Frenzy: One Year, Five Promising Students and the Pursuit of the Ivy League Prize*

"A long time ago, in an era far, far away, I took the SAT—and I can remember the pressure and anxiety of it like it was yesterday. Lucky for you modern-day seniors, Brian Leaf has written the SAT guide to end all SAT guides. He thoroughly demystifies the test and lays out the 50 skills you need to max out your score. Better yet, Mr. Leaf writes with such humor, wit, and unpretentious expertise that you'll find yourself reading this book just for fun. I did. It almost—almost—even made me want to take the SAT again."

Sora Song, Senior Editor, *Time Magazine*

"What's more scary than facing SATs? Or more boring than prepping for them? For a student swinging wildly between angst and ennui, the solution is Brian Leaf's *Top 50 Skills for a Top Score: SAT Critical Reading and Writing*. Leaf, himself a genius at connecting with teenagers, meets students at their level, and spikes every drill with common sense and comedy. I especially loved the Superbad Vocabulary section—not your usual stuffy approach to language deficit disorder. Guaranteed to relax and engage the most reluctant (or panicked) student."

Rebecca Pepper Sinkler, former Editor, *The New York Times Book Review*

Top 50 Skills for a Top Score: ACT Math

"Anyone even thinking of taking the ACT needs this short but targeted guide to the math section. You simply can't afford not to spend the time reading his laser sharp drills that break down every type of problem on the ACT, show the math behind each type, and then provide drill sections based on that skill set. Even poor math students can learn to recognize all the types of math on the ACT and learn the ropes enough to get most of the easy and medium questions right every time. Mr. Leaf's guide is even entertaining as he gives the skill sets names like "Green Circle, Black Diamond" to make it feel like you are skiing rather than slogging through lessons. If you want a short but concise guide to the ACT with every trick and mathematical explanation necessary to get a perfect score, this is the book for you. You may even actually LEARN real math in the process as Mr. Leaf's love of the subject shines through so you don't just feel you are learning for a test."

Dr. Michele Hernandez, author of the bestselling books *A is for Admission, The Middle School Years,* **and** *Acing the College Application*

"Brian Leaf knows how to talk with students and in his book, *Top 50 Skills for a Top Score: ACT Math*, you can hear his voice loud and clear. Students who follow Brian's "Mantras" and work through the practice questions will gain confidence in their work, as well as improve their ACT scores."

Barbara Anastos, former Director, Monmouth Academy

"Feels like you have an insider divulging secrets from behind the walls of the ACT! At times going so far as to circumvent the math skills themselves, Brian gives practical tips and tricks specifically designed to outwit the ACT's formula, and he does it all with a sense of humor and fun. Nice job!"

Danica McKellar, actress (*The Wonder Years, West Wing***) and mathematician and author of** *New York Times* **bestsellers** *Math Doesn't Suck* **and** *Kiss My Math*

Top 50 Skills for a Top Score: ACT English, Reading, and Science

"This book is a good read even if you *don't* have to take the ACT."

Edward Fiske, author of the bestselling college guide, the *Fiske Guide to Colleges*

"The **specific** skills needed for the ACT, confidence building, stress-management, how to avoid careless errors . . . this book has it covered!"

Laura Frey, Director of College Counseling, Vermont Academy
Former President, New England Association for College Admission Counseling

McGraw-Hill Education
Top 50 Skills for a Top Score:
SAT* Math

Second Edition

Brian Leaf, MA

New York | Chicago | San Francisco | Athens | London | Madrid |
Mexico City | Milan | New Delhi | Singapore | Sydney | Toronto

1 2 3 4 5 6 7 8 9   ROV   21 20 19 18 17 16

ISBN   978-1-2595-8567-8
MHID   1-2595-8567-0

e-ISBN   978-1-2595-8568-5
e-MHID   1-2595-8568-9

SAT is a registered trademark of the College Entrance Examination Board, which was not involved in the production of, and does not endorse, this product.

McGraw-Hill Education products are available at special quantity discounts to use as premiums and sales promotions, or for use in corporate training programs. To contact a representative, please visit Contact Us pages at www.mhprofessional.com.

Contents

How to Use This Book   vi
Easy, Medium, Hard, and Guessing   vii
About Brian Leaf, MA   viii
Acknowledgments   ix

Pretest   1

Top 50 Skills

Skill 1   Use the Answers   10
Skill 2   Algebraic Manipulation . . . "What
           Is p in Terms of f?"   12
Skill 3   "Mean" Means Average   14
Skill 4   The Six-Minute Abs of Geometry:
           Angles   16
Skill 5   The Six-Minute Abs of Geometry:
           Parallel Lines   18
Skill 6   The Six-Minute Abs of Geometry:
           Triangles   20
Skill 7   The Final Six-Minute Abs of Geometry   22
Skill 8   Math Vocab   24
Skill 9   More Math Vocab   26
Skill 10   Systems of Equations   28
Skill 11   Green Circle, Black Diamond:
           Slaloming Slope I   30
Skill 12   Green Circle, Black Diamond:
           Slaloming Slope II   32
Skill 13   The Sports Page: Using Tables
           and Graphs   34
Skill 14   Function Questions on the SAT, Type I   36
Skill 15   Function Questions on the SAT, Type II   38
Skill 16   Make It Real   40
Skill 17   Perimeter, Area, Volume   42
Skill 18   Donuts   44
Skill 19   Baking Granola Bars . . . Ratios   46
Skill 20   More Granola Bars . . . Proportions
           and Cross-Multiplying   48
Skill 21   Use the Diagram   50
Skill 22   Art Class   52
Skill 23   The Six-Minute Abs of Geometry:
           Length of a Side I   54
Skill 24   The Six-Minute Abs of Geometry:
           Length of a Side II   56
Skill 25   The Six-Minute Abs of Geometry:
           Length of a Side III   58
           Nina the Ninja, Let's Get Zen!
           A Yoga Posture for the SAT   60
           Guided Relaxation   61

Skill 26   "Is" Means Equals . . . Translation   62
Skill 27   Just Do It! . . . Springboard   64
Skill 28   Beyond Your Dear Aunt Sally:
           The Laws of Exponents I   66
Skill 29   Far Beyond Your Dear Aunt Sally:
           The Laws of Exponents II   68
Skill 30   Your Algebra Teacher Never Said
           "$y = ax + b$"   70
Skill 31   Arrangements   72
Skill 32   Long Word No-Problems   74
Skill 33   Tell Me What You Want, What You
           Really, Really Want . . . Probability   76
Skill 34   He's Making a List . . . Median,
           Mode, and Range   78
Skill 35 $y = ax^2 + bx + c$ 80
Skill 36   Circles   84
Skill 37   Hopscotch, Pigtails, and Remainders   86
Skill 38   Absolute Value   88
Skill 39   Sequences   90
Skill 40   Not So Complex Numbers   92
Skill 41   Don't Even Think About It! . . . Most
           Common SAT Math Careless Errors I   94
Skill 42   Don't Even Think About It! . . . Most
           Common SAT Math Careless Errors II   96
Skill 43   Misbehaving Numbers: Weird
           Number Behavior   98
Skill 44   Mathematical Transformations   100
Skill 45   SohCahToa!   102
Skill 46   Beyond SohCahToa   104
Skill 47   Directly and Inversely Proportional   106
Skill 48   Rational Expressions   110
Skill 49   How to Think Like a Math Genius I   112
Skill 50   How to Think Like a Math Genius II   116
           Brian's Friday Night Spiel:
           Recommendations for the Days
           Preceding the Test   120

Bonus Skill: Hello Harvard . . . How
to Break 700   122
Easy, Medium, Hard, and Guessing Revisited   123
Now What?   124
Posttest I   125
Solutions   135
Glossary   164
Top 50 Skills Flash Cards

How to Use This Book

It's simple. The questions that will appear on your SAT are predictable. Every SAT has a few function questions, one or two ratio questions, an average question, etc. While each of these topics is broad and could be the subject of a whole mathematics course, **the SAT always tests the same concepts!**

In this book, I will teach you exactly what you need to know. I will introduce each topic and follow it with drills. After each set of drills, check your answers. Read and reread the solutions until they make sense. They are designed to simulate one-on-one tutoring, like I'm sitting right there with you. Reread the solutions until you could teach them to a friend. In fact, do that! My students call it "learning to channel their inner Brian Leaf." There is no better way to learn and master a concept than to teach it!

Any new concept that you master will be worth 10 or more points toward you SAT Math score. That's the plan; it is that simple. If you did not understand functions, ratios, and averages before and now you do, you will earn 30+ extra points.

This book is filled with SAT Math Mantras. They tell you what to do and when to do it. "When you see a proportion, cross-multiply." "When you see a linear pair, determine the measures of the angles." This is the stuff that girl who got a perfect score on her SAT Math does automatically. The Mantras teach you to think like her.

"Sounds good, but the SAT is tricky," you say. It is, but we know their tricks. Imagine a football team that has great plays, but only a few of them. We could watch films and study those plays. No matter how tricky they are, we could learn them, expect them, and beat them. SAT prep works the same way. You will learn the strategies, expect the SAT's tricks, and raise your score. Now, go learn and rack up the points!

Easy, Medium, Hard, and Guessing

The SAT is not graded like a math test at school. If you got only half the questions right on an algebra midterm, that'd be a big fat F. On the math SAT, half the questions right is a 500, the average score for kids across the country. If you got 70% of the questions right, that'd be a C– in school, but almost a 600 on the SAT, the average score for admission to schools like Goucher and University of Vermont. If you got 89% correct, which is a measly B+ in school, it is a beautiful 700 on the SAT, and about the average for kids who got into Georgetown, U.C. Berkeley, Emory, and Wesleyan.

Use this info to determine how many questions you need to answer on the SAT. The math questions are organized in order of difficulty, from easiest to hardest. If you want half correct, or 70% correct, don't rush through the easies just to get to the hard ones. In school you might need to finish tests in order to do well, here you do not. You only need to get to the very hardest questions if you are shooting for 700+.

In this book, the drills that follow each skill are also arranged easiest to hardest. Knowing the level of difficulty of a question is important. The easy questions are worth just as much as the hard ones. So, don't rush and risk a careless error just to reach the hard questions. If an easy or medium question seems hard, take another look for what you are missing. Ask yourself, "Which skill can I use? What is the easy way to do this question?" After you complete this book, you will know! What about guessing? Well, you do not lose points for wrong answers, so put an answer for every question, even ones that you do not get to. Even if you are running out of time, budget a bit of time to fill in an answer for the last questions. It'd be crazy not to. Statistically, if you randomly fill in the last four ovals, you'll get one correct. That could be worth 10 points on your score! So keep an eye on the clock, and when there are a few minutes left, choose an answer for each remaining question.

About Brian Leaf, MA

Six, maybe seven, people in the world know the SAT like Brian Leaf. Most are under surveillance in Princeton, NJ. Brian alone is left to bring you this book.

Brian has seen the SAT from every angle, even teaching yoga to the test makers at ETS Corporation. You are about to find out what Brian learned from them while they slept in deep relaxation.

Brian is the author of *McGraw-Hill's Top 50 Skills* SAT and ACT test-prep series and the Director of the *New Leaf Learning Center* in Western Massachusetts. He teaches SAT, PSAT, and ACT prep to thousands of students from throughout the United States. (For more information, visit his website www.BrianLeaf.com.) Brian also works with the Georgetown University Office of Undergraduate Admissions as an Alumni Interviewer. For more about Brian, check out his hilarious memoir, *Misadventures of a Garden State Yogi*.

Acknowledgments

Special thanks to all the students of New Leaf Learning Center for allowing me to find this book. Thanks to my agent Linda Roghaar and my Editor at McGraw-Hill, Anya Kozorez. Thanks Pam Weber-Leaf for great editing tips; Larry Leaf for his one-liners; Zach Nelson for sage marketing advice; Ben Allison, Jake Duggan, and Sarah Duggan for their math genius and thorough editing; Matthew Thompson for astute design help; Susan and Manny Leaf for everything; and of course, thanks most of all to Gwen, Noah, and Benji for time, love, support, and, in the case of Benji, an uncanny ability to locate treasure.

Pretest

The following 50 questions correspond to our 50 Skills. Take the test, and then check your answers in the 50 Skill sections that follow.

DIRECTIONS: This pretest contains the two types of math questions that you will see on the SAT: multiple-choice and student-produced response questions. Multiple-choice questions are followed by answer choices. Solve each and decide which is the best of the choices given. Student-produced response questions are not followed by answer choices.

You may use any available space for scratchwork. A calculator is permitted unless you see the symbol.

 1 If m is a positive integer and $\dfrac{m+1}{3^2} = \dfrac{1}{3}$, what is the value of m?

(A) −1

(B) 0

(C) 1

(D) 2

2 If $4x + 2y = 12$, what is y in terms of x?

(A) $6 + 2x$

(B) $6 - 2x$

(C) $12 - 4x$

(D) $12 - 2x$

3 If the average (arithmetic mean) of m and n is 7, what is $m + n$?

(A) 3.5

(B) 7

(C) 14

(D) 21

4 In the figure below, what is the value of a?

(A) 25

(B) 30

(C) 35

(D) 40

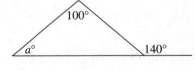

5 In the figure below, if $a \parallel b$ and the measure of $x = 45$, what is the measure of y?

Ⓐ 27
Ⓑ 53
Ⓒ 127
Ⓓ 153

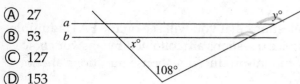

6 If $MN = MO$ in the figure below, which of the following must be true?

Ⓐ $a = b$
Ⓑ $b = c$
Ⓒ $a = c$
Ⓓ $MN = NO$

Note: Figure not drawn to scale.

7 In the figure below, what is the value of b?

Ⓐ 50
Ⓑ 55
Ⓒ 60
Ⓓ 65

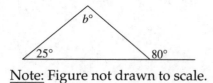

Note: Figure not drawn to scale.

(Question 8 is the first example in this book of an SAT student-produced response question, where you are not given multiple-choice options and must come up with your own answer.)

8 Let S equal the set of all real numbers. How many members of S are even prime numbers?

9 If P is the set of all <u>different</u>, real number, prime factors of 100, how many members does set P contain?

Ⓐ None
Ⓑ 2
Ⓒ 3
Ⓓ 8

$$-2x = 8y + 6$$
$$-3(2y + 4) = 4x - 14$$

10 What is the x-value of the solution (x, y) to the system of equations above?

11 If the slope of a line through the points (2, 4) and (0, *b*) is 1, what is the value of *b*?

(A) −2

(B) −1

(C) 1

(D) 2

12 In the *xy* coordinate plane, line *j* is the reflection of line *k* about the *x*-axis. If the slope of line *j* is $\frac{-3}{4}$, what is the slope of line *k*?

(A) $\frac{4}{3}$

(B) $\frac{3}{4}$

(C) $\frac{1}{4}$

(D) $\frac{-3}{4}$

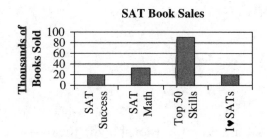

SAT Book Sales

13 According to the graph above, which two SAT books sold the fewest copies?

(A) SAT Math and I ♥ SATs

(B) I ♥ SATs and Top 50 Skills

(C) I ♥ SATs and SAT Success

(D) SAT Success and SAT Math

14 If *f*(*x*) = 2*x* + 1, what is *f*(3)?

15 If *f*(*x*) = 2*x* + 1 and *f*(*m*) = 9, what is *m*?

16 Grandma Jones is making cookies for the fair. She needs *x* cups of flour per batch. Each batch makes *c* number of cookies. If she has 10 cups of flour, in terms of *x* and *c*, how many cookies can she make?

(A) *xc*

(B) 10*xc*

(C) $\frac{10c}{x}$

(D) $\frac{10x}{c}$

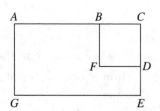

17 In the figure above, the perimeter of square *BCDF* is 12, and the perimeter of rectangle *ACEG* is 30. If *AB* and *DE* are each positive integers, what is one possible value of the area of rectangle *ACEG*?

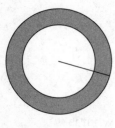

18 In the diagram above, if the area of the large circle is 10 and the area of the small circle is 8, what is the area of the shaded region?

19 In a mixture of pretzels and corn chips, the ratio of pretzels to corn chips is 3 to 7. How many pretzels will be in a mixture that has 100 total pieces?

Ⓐ 70

Ⓑ 50

Ⓒ 37

Ⓓ 30

20 If the numerator of a fraction is 3 more than the denominator, and the fraction equals $\frac{4}{3}$, what is the numerator of the fraction?

Ⓐ 3

Ⓑ 6

Ⓒ 9

Ⓓ 12

21 In the figure below, *ABED* is a square with sides of length 6. If *EC* = 3, what is the perimeter of quadrilateral *ABCD*?

Ⓐ 24

Ⓑ 27

Ⓒ $18 + 3\sqrt{5}$

Ⓓ $21 + 3\sqrt{5}$

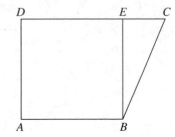

22 Points *A*, *B*, *C*, *D*, and *E* are collinear. If *B* is the midpoint of $\overline{AC}$, *C* is the midpoint of $\overline{AD}$, and *D* is the midpoint of $\overline{AE}$, which of the following is the longest segment?

Ⓐ $\overline{AB}$

Ⓑ $\overline{AD}$

Ⓒ $\overline{BC}$

Ⓓ $\overline{CE}$

Note: Figure not drawn to scale.

23 In right triangle *ABC* (not shown), the measure of *AB* is 6 and the measure of *BC* is 10. Which of the following could be the measure of *AC*?

Ⓐ 3

Ⓑ 4

Ⓒ 6

Ⓓ 8

24 If triangle *MNO* (not shown) is congruent to triangle *PQR* shown below, which of the following is the measure of longest side of triangle *MNO*?

Ⓐ 3

Ⓑ $3\sqrt{3}$

Ⓒ 6

Ⓓ $6\sqrt{3}$

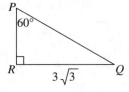

25 If triangle *MNO* (not shown) is similar to triangle *PQR* shown below, and has a shortest side with length 4.5, which of the following could be the measure of the longest side of triangle *MNO*?

Ⓐ 4.5

Ⓑ 6.5

Ⓒ 9

Ⓓ 12

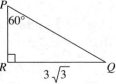

26 If 20 percent of 10 percent of a number is 24 less than half the number, what is the number?

27 If $x^2 - y^2 = 36$ and $x - y = 12$, what is the value of $x + y$?

28 If *m*, *n*, and *p* are positive integers and $3^m \cdot 3^n \cdot 3^p = 81$, then the greatest possible value for *p* is

Ⓐ 1

Ⓑ 2

Ⓒ 3

Ⓓ 4

29 If $8m^2p^3 = m^5p$, what is *m* in terms of *p*?

Ⓐ $p^{2/3}$

Ⓑ $2p^{2/3}$

Ⓒ $8p^{2/3}$

Ⓓ $2p^2$

30 If McLovin's lawn-mowing service charges $25 to come to a house and $0.50 for each bag of leaves that they remove, which of the following equations express McLovin's fees for a visit if they remove *x* bags of leaves?

Ⓐ $y = 25$

Ⓑ $y = 25x + 0.5$

Ⓒ $y = 0.5x$

Ⓓ $y = 0.5x + 25$

31 Fletch F. Fletch buys an ice cream sundae that contains one scoop of ice cream, one sauce, and either a cherry or pineapple wedge on top. He can choose chocolate, vanilla, strawberry, or banana ice cream; he can choose chocolate, caramel, or berry sauce; and he can choose either the cherry or the pineapple wedge for the top. How many different arrangements of these ingredients for Fletch's ice cream sundae are possible?

$A = P(1 + r)^{tn}$

32 The formula above is used to calculate compound interest. A represents the amount of money accumulated after n years including interest, P is the initial principal amount (i.e., the initial amount deposited), r stands for the annual rate of interest as a decimal, and t represents the number of years and n the number of times the interest is compounded per year. If Sal deposits $100 in an account earning 6% annual interest and keeps the money in his account for five years, how much money will he have at the end of the five years? Round your answer to the nearest dollar.

Ⓐ 30
Ⓑ 130
Ⓒ 133
Ⓓ 134

33 Of the 24 chocolates in a box, 10 are solid milk chocolate, 10 are solid dark chocolate, and 4 are cream-filled. If Noah randomly chooses a chocolate from the box, what is the probability that it will NOT be solid dark chocolate?

Ⓐ $\dfrac{1}{12}$

Ⓑ $\dfrac{1}{6}$

Ⓒ $\dfrac{5}{12}$

Ⓓ $\dfrac{7}{12}$

34 The median of a set of nine consecutive integers is 42. What is the greatest of these nine numbers?

35 If the graph of $y = ax^2 + bx + c$ is shown below, then the value of ac could be

I. Positive
II. Negative
III. 0

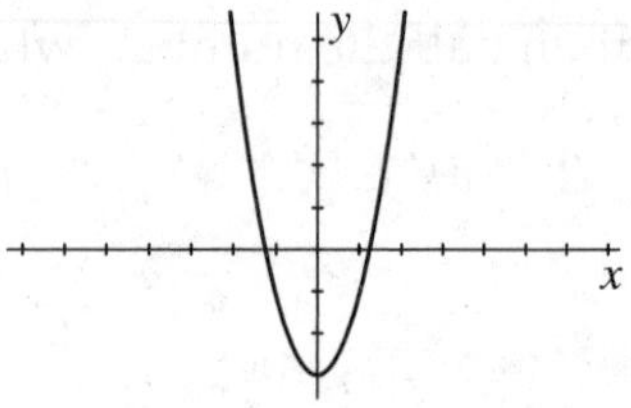

Ⓐ I only
Ⓑ II only
Ⓒ I or II
Ⓓ I or III

36 A circle in the standard (x, y) coordinate plane has center $(4, 2)$ and radius 5 coordinate units. Which of the following is an equation of the circle?

- (A) $(x - 4)^2 - (y - 2)^2 = 5$
- (B) $(x + 4)^2 + (y + 2)^2 = 5$
- (C) $(x - 4)^2 + (y - 2)^2 = 25$
- (D) $(x - 4)^2 + (y + 2)^2 = 25$

37 All the following numbers have remainder 3 when divided by 4 EXCEPT

- (A) 7
- (B) 15
- (C) 22
- (D) 23

38 Which of the following are solutions to $|n + 3| = 5$?

   I. 2

   II. -2

   III. -8

- (A) I only
- (B) III only
- (C) II and III
- (D) I and III

39 Which of the following is NOT true about the arithmetic sequence 20, 13, 6, -1, . . . ?

- (A) The fifth term is -8.
- (B) The sum of the first five terms is 30.
- (C) The common ratio of consecutive terms is -7.
- (D) The seventh term is -22.

40 What is $(i - 2)(i - 3)$?

- (A) $5 - 5i$
- (B) $5 - 4i$
- (C) $5 + i$
- (D) 5

41 If $f(x) = 3x^2$, which of the following expresses $f(2p)$?

- (A) $6p$
- (B) $6p^2$
- (C) $12p$
- (D) $12p^2$

42 For the equation $y = -3x^3 - 2$, when $x = 1$, what is the value of $-2y$?

43 If $0.5mno = 0$ and $4nop = 12$, then which of the following must be true?

Ⓐ $nop = 12$

Ⓑ $mno = -0.5$

Ⓒ $p = 0$

Ⓓ $m = 0$

44 The graph of $y = g(x)$ is shown below. Which of the following equations represents all the points of $g(x)$ shifted 1 unit to the left?

Ⓐ $y = g(x) + 1$

Ⓑ $y = g(x + 1)$

Ⓒ $y = g(x - 1)$

Ⓓ $y = g(x) - 1$

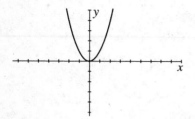

45 For right triangle $\triangle XYZ$, in which the lengths of XY, YZ, and XZ are 3, 4, and 5, respectively, what is $\tan Z$?

Ⓐ 0.2

Ⓑ 0.6

Ⓒ 0.75

Ⓓ 0.8

46 What is the value of θ, between 0 and 360, when $\sin \theta = -1$?

Ⓐ 0

Ⓑ 60

Ⓒ 135

Ⓓ 270

47 If y is directly proportional to x^3 and $y = 64$ when $x = 2$, what is x when $y = 216$?

48 $\dfrac{3x+9}{x-3} + \dfrac{x+2}{x+3} =$

Ⓐ $\dfrac{4x+11}{x^2-9}$

Ⓑ $\dfrac{3x^2+121}{(x-3)(x+3)}$

Ⓒ $\dfrac{4x^2+17x+21}{(x-3)(x+3)}$

Ⓓ $\dfrac{4x^2+21}{x^2-9}$

Movie	Votes
Superbad	♥ ♥ ♥ ♥ ♥
Borat	♥ ❧
Wedding Crashers	♥ ❧
Godfather	♥

♥ = 10 votes

 49 The table above shows the results of a survey in which 90 high school students voted for their favorite movie. Each student received one vote. According to the graph, how many more students favored *Superbad* than favored *Borat*?

Ⓐ 3

Ⓑ 3.5

Ⓒ 35

Ⓓ 39.5

50 Ahmed is both the 7th tallest and 7th shortest student in class. If everyone is a different height, how many students total are in the class?

BONUS QUESTION

The night before the SAT you should

Ⓐ eat 2 pounds of pasta for runner's endurance energy

Ⓑ eat two whole live lobsters for omega-3 fatty acids

Ⓒ have a huge pre-SAT party

Ⓓ relax and sleep well

Use the Answers

For 11 years you've been trained to solve math problems the long way. "No shortcuts!" Mrs. Nicholas always said. Mrs. Nicholas was the best math teacher that I ever had, and her advice was correct for math class. But the SAT is multiple choice, and we can save time and energy by using the answers. Instead of completing a long process of algebraic manipulation, simply test the answer choices to see which one works. This strategy works best when there are **variables** in the question and **numbers** in the answer choices.

Let's look at the question from the Pretest:

1. If m is a positive integer and $\dfrac{m+1}{3^2} = \dfrac{1}{3}$, what is the value of m?

   (A) −1   (B) 0   (C) 1   (D) 2

Solution: This question looks pretty tough to some students, but "Use the Answers" makes it EASY! Just plug each answer choice in for m to see which one makes the equation work. Choice A does not work because when we plug −1 in for m in the equation, we get $\dfrac{-1+1}{3^2} = \dfrac{0}{9} = 0$ instead of $\dfrac{1}{3}$. Choice D is the only one that works, since $\dfrac{2+1}{3^2} = \dfrac{3}{9} = \dfrac{1}{3}$.

Correct answer: D

SAT Math Mantra #1
**When you see <u>variables</u> in the question and <u>numbers</u> in the answers,
"Use the Answers."**

Use the Answers Drills

Easy

 1 If $2x - 3 = 17$, then $x =$

   Ⓐ −1

   Ⓑ 0

   Ⓒ 10

   Ⓓ 22

2 For which of the following values of p will the value of $4p + 2$ be less than 15 ?

   Ⓐ 7

   Ⓑ 6

   Ⓒ 4

   Ⓓ 3

Medium

3 If j is a positive integer and $\dfrac{j+1}{2^3} = \dfrac{1}{2}$, what is the value of j ?

   Ⓐ 0

   Ⓑ 1

   Ⓒ 3

   Ⓓ 4

4 If $|\,3 - n\,| < 4$, which of the following is a possible value of n ?

   Ⓐ 9

   Ⓑ 8

   Ⓒ 7

   Ⓓ 6

5 What value of t would make $\sqrt{\dfrac{-2(t)}{3}} = 6$?

   Ⓐ −54

   Ⓑ −27

   Ⓒ 0

   Ⓓ 27

Hard

6 The cost, in dollars, of production for u units at Max's factory is expressed by the function $P(u) = 500\left(\dfrac{6}{5}\right)$. If Max can spend \$7300 on production, what is the maximum number of units he can produce?

   Ⓐ 1

   Ⓑ 2

   Ⓒ 3

   Ⓓ 4

SAT Myth Busters

Myth: Algebraic manipulation was invented in the dungeons of medieval Europe, a brutal byzantine torture.

Fact: Algebraic manipulation was actually invented in ancient Greece and was not used for torture until the mid-1900s.

Students often come into my office and say, "This question says, 'What is m in terms of p and q' and I have no idea what that means, so I skipped it." I love these, because they are so easy to teach and to gain points with. "What is m in terms of p and q" is just a fancy way of saying "solve for m" or "use algebra to get m alone." Whatever letter is after the "what is . . ." is the variable that you solve for. That's it, and every SAT has several of these questions!

Let's take a look at the Pretest:

2. If $4x + 2y = 12$, what is y in terms of x?

(A) $6 + 2x$ (B) $6 - 2x$ (C) $12 - 4x$ (D) $12 - 2x$

Solution: Just use algebra to get y alone.

$$4x + 2y = 12$$
$$\underline{-4x \qquad\quad -4x} \qquad \text{subtract } 4x \text{ from both sides}$$
$$2y = 12 - 4x \qquad \text{divide both sides by 2}$$
$$y = 6 - 2x$$

Correct answer: B

SAT Math Mantra #2
"What is m in terms of p and q" is just a fancy way of saying
"solve for m" or "use algebra to get m alone."

Easy

 1 If $D = RT$, what is R in terms of D and T ?

Ⓐ DT

Ⓑ $D - T$

Ⓒ $\dfrac{T}{D}$

Ⓓ $\dfrac{D}{T}$

Medium

 2 If $3m = 2n$ and $2n = 4p$, what is m in terms of p ?

Ⓐ $\dfrac{3p}{4}$

Ⓑ $\dfrac{4p}{3}$

Ⓒ $12p$

Ⓓ $24p$

Hard

3 If $x + 3(b - 1) = k$, what is $b - 1$ in terms of x and k ?

Ⓐ $\dfrac{k}{3} - x$

Ⓑ $\dfrac{k - x}{3}$

Ⓒ $\dfrac{k + x}{3}$

Ⓓ $\dfrac{kx}{3}$

4 If p and q are positive and $5p^3q^{-2} = 25p^2$, what does p^{-1} equal in terms of q?

Ⓐ $\dfrac{q^L}{5}$

Ⓑ $\dfrac{5}{q^2}$

Ⓒ $25q^2$

Ⓓ $\dfrac{1}{5q^2}$

5 Leaf's Law states that $L = \sqrt{2x}\ \dfrac{p}{5q^2}$ where p represents price per SAT book and q represents quantity of books purchased in bulk and x represents the number of years after 2016. Which of the following expresses p in terms of L, q, and x?

Ⓐ $p = 5q^2 L\sqrt{2x}$

Ⓑ $p = \dfrac{5q^2 L}{\sqrt{2x}}$

Ⓒ $p = \dfrac{q^2 L\sqrt{2x}}{5}$

Ⓓ $p = \dfrac{q^2 \sqrt{2x}}{5L}$

"Mean" Means Average

This is one of my favorite SAT strategies. It's true, I have favorite SAT strategies, but it's just such a good one and makes average questions so much easier.

The "average" of a list of numbers is found by adding them and dividing by how many there are.

$$\text{Average} = \frac{\text{sum}}{\text{number of items}}$$

This is very simple, and the SAT knows that you have been figuring out your grade point average, test average, or bowling average for years. Therefore, they do not usually ask you only to find the average of a list of numbers; they say, "Given the average, find the sum of the numbers." This gets kids, but if you know the strategy, it's easy! Just know this formula:

$$\text{Sum} = (\text{average}) \times (\text{number of items})$$

This is the key to unlock almost any average question on the SAT. As soon as you see the word "mean" or "average" on the test, consider using this formula. By the way, sometimes when the SAT prints the word "average," they follow it with "(arithmetic mean)." This is simply a clarification and a synonym for "average." They are just referring to the normal average that you are used to, so ignore "(arithmetic mean)."

Let's look at the question from the Pretest:

3. If the average (arithmetic mean) of m and n is 7, what is $m + n$?

   (A) 3.5   (B) 7   (C) 14   (D) 21

Solution: For an average question, we use either the average formula or the sum formula. How do you know which? The question asks for one or the other! This question asks for the sum, so set up the sum formula:

Sum = (average) × (number of items)

$(m + n) = 7 \times 2 = 14$

Correct answer: C

SAT Math Mantra #3
When you see the word "average" on the SAT,
use sum = (average) × (number of items).

"Mean" Means Average Drills

Medium

1 If the average (arithmetic mean) of m and $4m$ is 30, what is the value of m ?

- (A) 4
- (B) 6
- (C) 10
- (D) 12

2 The average (arithmetic mean) of the scores of 21 students on an exam is k. In terms of k, what is the sum of the scores of all 21 students?

- (A) $21 + k$
- (B) $21k$
- (C) $\dfrac{k}{21}$
- (D) $\dfrac{21}{k}$

3 The average (arithmetic mean) of m and n is 7, and the average of m, n, and p is 11. What is the value of p ?

- (A) 31
- (B) 29
- (C) 21
- (D) 19

4 If the perimeters of two shapes have a sum of 9, what is the average (arithmetic mean) of the perimeters of the two shapes?

- (A) 0
- (B) $\dfrac{2}{9}$
- (C) $\dfrac{9}{4}$
- (D) $\dfrac{9}{2}$

5 The average (arithmetic mean) of the test scores of a class of 20 students is 80, and the average of the scores of a class of 30 students is 92. What is the average of both classes combined?

- (A) 25
- (B) 86
- (C) 87.2
- (D) 89.5

6 The average (arithmetic mean) of m, n, o, and p is 55. If the average of m, n, o, p, and q is 70, what is the value of q ?

Hard

7 Each of five judges had a scorecard on which they wrote a different positive integer. If the average (arithmetic mean) of these integers is 7, what is the greatest possible integer that could be on one of the cards?

The Six-Minute Abs of Geometry: Angles

Every SAT has a bunch of geometry questions. Many students panic, "I don't remember the million stupid postulates we learned." Good news, you only need a small handful of those million postulates to solve most geometry questions.

Skills 4 through 7 show you how to find the measure of an angle in a diagram. Every SAT has several of these questions; memorize these skills and you will gain points, guaranteed.

1 Vertical angles are equal.

$a° = b°$

2 The angles in a linear pair add up to 180°.

$m + n = 180°$

If you are given m, then $n = 180 - m$.

3 The angles in a triangle add up to 180°.
The angles in a four-sided shape add up to 360°.
The angles in a five-sided shape add up to 540°.
The angles in a six-sided shape add up to 720°.

$x + y + z = 180°$

Now, let's look at the question from the Pretest.

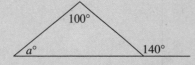

4. In the figure above, what is the value of a ?

  (A) 25   (B) 30   (C) 35   (D) 40

Solution: This question uses two of our strategies: linear pair and 180° in a triangle. As soon as you see a linear pair of angles, determine the measures of the angles in the pair. So the angle next to the 140° must be 180° − 140° = 40°. Now we have two of three angles in a triangle which must add up to 180°, so the third must be 180° − 100° − 40° = 40°.

Correct answer: D

```
Math Mantra #4
When you see vertical angles, a linear pair, or a triangle,
calculate the measures of all angles.
```

Easy

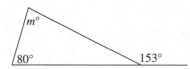

1 In the figure above, what is the value of m?

- Ⓐ 150
- Ⓑ 80
- Ⓒ 73
- Ⓓ 27

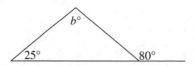

Note: Figure not drawn to scale.

2 In the figure above, what is the value of b ?

- Ⓐ 50
- Ⓑ 55
- Ⓒ 60
- Ⓓ 65

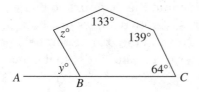

3 If $y = 60$ and points A, B, and C lie on the same line, what is the value of z ?

- Ⓐ 125
- Ⓑ 100
- Ⓒ 84
- Ⓓ 62

Medium

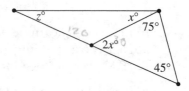

Note: Figure not drawn to scale.

4 In the figure above, what is the value of z ?

Hard

5 In the figure above, if AB is a line, what is n in terms of m ?

- Ⓐ $180 - m$
- Ⓑ $180 - 2m$
- Ⓒ $\dfrac{180 - m}{2}$
- Ⓓ $\dfrac{180 - 2m}{3}$

The Six-Minute Abs of Geometry: Parallel Lines

In math class, learning about parallel lines can seem pretty tricky—alternate interior angles, corresponding angles, same-side interior angles. . . . We don't need all that for the SAT. We just need to know that

- Parallel lines are two lines that never touch.
- If two parallel lines are crossed by another line (called a transversal), then eight angles form.
- These eight angles are of two types, big or little. All bigs are equal, and all littles are equal.

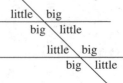

This is enough to answer any parallel lines SAT question.
There's another 10 points!

Now, let's take a look at the question from the Pretest.

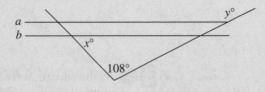

5. In the figure above, if $a \parallel b$ and the measure of $x = 45$, what is the measure of y ?

(A) 27   (B) 53   (C) 127   (D) 153

Solution: First, always mark any info from the question into the diagram, so mark $x = 45$. Remember SAT Math Mantra #4. When you are given two angles of a triangle, always determine the third, so $180° - 108° - 45° = 27°$. Next, in the pair of parallel lines, there are only two kinds of angles, big and little. Angle y is big, not little, so it equals $180° - 27° = 153°$.

Correct answer: D

SAT Math Mantra #5
When you see two parallel lines that are crossed by another line,
eight angles are formed, and all the bigger-looking angles are equal,
and all the smaller-looking angles are equal.

Easy

1 In the figure below, $m \parallel n$. If $y = 45$, what is the value of x?

Ⓐ 45
Ⓑ 100
Ⓒ 135
Ⓓ 145

2 If $x = 66$ and $p \parallel q$ and $m \parallel n$ in the four lines shown, what is the value of z?

Ⓐ 24
Ⓑ 66
Ⓒ 90
Ⓓ 114

3 In the figure below, $m \parallel n$. If $z = 40$ and $x = 130$, then $y =$

Ⓐ 90
Ⓑ 80
Ⓒ 40
Ⓓ 50

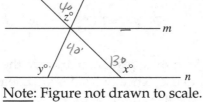

Note: Figure not drawn to scale.

Medium

4 If $z = 45$ and $y = 95$ in the figure below, then which of the following must be true?

Ⓐ $p \parallel q$
Ⓑ $x + y = 180$
Ⓒ $z = x$
Ⓓ $x + z = 180$

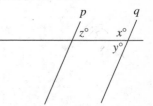

Note: Figure not drawn to scale.

5 In the figure below, if $a \parallel b$ and the measure of $x = 22$, what is the measure of y?

Ⓐ 22
Ⓑ 50
Ⓒ 108
Ⓓ 130

Note: Figure not drawn to scale.

The Six-Minute Abs of Geometry: Triangles

Sir Bedevere: . . . and that, my liege, is how we know the Earth to be banana shaped.

King Arthur: This new learning amazes me, Sir Bedevere. Explain again how sheep's bladders may be employed to prevent earthquakes.

Monty Python and the Holy Grail (20th Century Fox, 1975)

Back in geometry class, you had a full chapter with 14 theorems classifying triangles. Here are two that matter for the SAT.

 1 If a triangle is isosceles (a fancy term for having two equal sides), then the two angles opposite the equal sides are also equal.

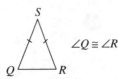

2 If a triangle is equilateral (a fancy term for having all sides equal), then it has all equal angles of 60° each.

Let's take a look at the question from the Pretest.

Note: Figure not drawn to scale.

6. If *MN* = *MO* in the figure above, which of the following must be true?

(A) *a* = *b*   (B) *b* = *c*   (C) *a* = *c*   (D) *MN* = *NO*

Solution: As soon as you are given info in the question, mark it in the diagram. This will remind you which geometry skill to use. Since two sides are equal in the triangle, the two angles opposite the two sides are also equal. So *b* = *c*.

Correct answer: B

SAT Math Mantra #6
When you see a triangle with two equal sides, mark the two opposite angles as equal, and when all sides of a triangle are equal, mark all angles 60°.

Easy

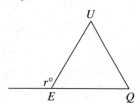

1 If triangle *EQU*, shown above, is equilateral, what is the value of *r* ?

Ⓐ 30

Ⓑ 60

Ⓒ 90

Ⓓ 120

2 If *MN = ON* in the figure above, and *b* = 43, what is the value of *c*?

Ⓐ 43

Ⓑ 68.5

Ⓒ 75.5

Ⓓ 137

Medium

Note: Figure not drawn to scale.

3 If triangle *ABC*, shown above, has the perimeter of 21, and if *AC = AB =* 7, what is the value of ∠*ACB* ?

Ⓐ 7°

Ⓑ 14°

Ⓒ 30°

Ⓓ 60°

Note: Figure not drawn to scale.

4 If the area of right triangle *MNO* is 72, and the measure of *MO* is 12, what is the value of ∠*MON* ?

Ⓐ 15°

Ⓑ 30°

Ⓒ 45°

Ⓓ 72°

The Final Six-Minute Abs of Geometry

By the end of this Skill, you will have learned all that you need to know about angles for the SAT. That's great news because **every** SAT includes several angle questions, and now you can always get them right. You know what to expect, you know what to use, and you will earn 30 or more points!

Here are the last two concepts for finding an angle:

❶ An exterior angle equals the sum of the two far-away interior angles.

$x = a + b$

❷ "Bisect" means to cut into two equal parts. An angle bisector cuts an angle into two equal parts, and a segment bisector cuts a segment into two equal parts.

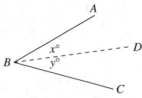

Segment *BD* bisects angle *ABC*.
It cuts it into two equal parts, so $x = y$.

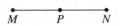

Point *P* bisects segment *MN*.
It is the midpoint and cuts the segment into two equal parts, so $MP = PN$.

Now, let's take a look at the question from the Pretest.

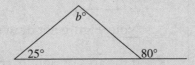

Note: Figure not drawn to scale.

7. In the figure above, what is the value of *b*?

  (A) 50   (B) 55   (C) 60   (D) 65

Solution: This is essentially a question from Skill 4, but this time we know the exterior angle trick. Since an exterior angle equals the sum of the two far-away interior angles, $80 = 25 + b$. So $b = 55$.

Correct answer: B

SAT Math Mantra #7
An exterior angle equals the sum of the two far-away interior angles.

The Final Six-Minute Abs of Geometry Drills

Medium

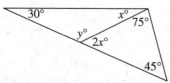

Note: Figure not drawn to scale.

1 In the figure above, what is the value of $y - x$?

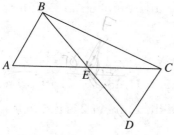

Note: Figure not drawn to scale.

2 In the figure above, segments AC and BD intersect at E. If the measure of $\angle AEB$ is 70° and segment EF (not shown) bisects $\angle BEC$, what is the measure of $\angle FED$?

Hard

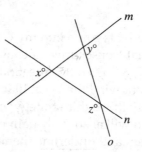

3 In the figure above, if $x = 71$, what is the value of $y + z$?

Ⓐ 71

Ⓑ 142

Ⓒ 211

Ⓓ 251

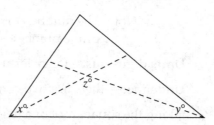

4 In the figure above, the dotted lines bisect angles with measures $x°$ and $y°$. In terms of x and y, what is the value of z?

Ⓐ $180 - 0.5(x + y)$

Ⓑ $0.5(x + y)$

Ⓒ $180 - (x + y)$

Ⓓ $180 + (x - y)$

Students come into my office and say, "I can't do this question because I don't know what 'consecutive' means." I get to say, "Oh cool, it just means numbers in a row, like 4, 5, 6." Then the question becomes easy. In fact, for some questions, the only hard part is knowing the vocabulary, and once you know the terms, the questions are easy. That's why I love this strategy; memorize these terms and practice using them in the drills, and you will absolutely gain points, guaranteed. Also, once you know the terms, watch for them and <u>underline</u> them when they appear. That will eliminate many careless errors. Here are nine math vocabulary terms:

Real number—any number on the SAT except for i, such as: $-3, -2.2, 0, \sqrt{2}, \pi$.

Constant term—this term really throws some kids, but it just means a letter in place of a number, kinda like a variable, except that it won't vary.

Integer—number without decimals or fractions: $-3, -2, -1, 0, 1, 2, 3, \ldots$. This is the single most common SAT math vocab word!

Even/odd—even numbers: $2, 4, 6, 8, \ldots$; odd numbers: $1, 3, 5, 7, \ldots$.

Positive/negative—positive numbers are greater than 0; negative numbers are less than 0.

Consecutive numbers—numbers in a row: 7, 8, 9, 10.

Different numbers—numbers that are . . . ummm . . . different.

Prime—a number whose only factors are 1 and itself. $2, 3, 5, 7, 11, 13, 17, \ldots$ are prime.

> <u>Note</u>: The number 1 is NOT considered prime, and the number 2 is the *only* even prime number.

Units digit—just a fancy term for the "ones" digit in a number, like the 2 in 672.

Undefined—there are two conditions that make a mathematical expression undefined: taking the square root of a negative number and dividing by zero, so $\sqrt{-5}$ and $\frac{2x}{0}$ are undefined.

Let's take a look at the question from the Pretest.

8. Let S equal the set of all real numbers. How many members of S are even prime numbers?

Solution: List the primes: 2, 3, 5, 7, 11, 13, 17, 19, 23. Only the number 2 is prime and even. No other primes can be even, since every even number (besides the number 2) has factors other than 1 and itself.

Correct answer: 1

+--+
| **SAT Math Mantra #8** |
| **Anytime you see a math vocab term, underline it.** |
+--+

Math Vocab Drills

Easy

 1 If two consecutive integers have a sum of 9, what is the larger number?

2 How many different integers satisfy the equation $x^2 = 9$?

Ⓐ 0
Ⓑ 1
Ⓒ 2
Ⓓ 3

3 How many positive integers less than 100 have a units digit of 3?

Ⓐ 100
Ⓑ 50
Ⓒ 12
Ⓓ 10

Medium

4 If two consecutive prime numbers have a sum of 60, what is the larger number?

5 Two consecutive even integers have a sum of −26. Which of the following **must** be true?

   I. Both numbers are negative.

   II. The lesser number is −12.

   III. The lesser number is −14.

Ⓐ I only.
Ⓑ II only.
Ⓒ I and III only.
Ⓓ II and III only.

6 For what value(s) of x is the following expression undefined?

$$\sqrt{2x-5}$$

Ⓐ $x = 5$
Ⓑ $x = \dfrac{5}{2}$
Ⓒ $x < \dfrac{5}{2}$
Ⓓ $x \leq 5$

7 For what value(s) of x is the following expression undefined?

$$\frac{2x}{(x-3)(x+4)}$$

Ⓐ 0
Ⓑ 3
Ⓒ 3, −4
Ⓓ 0, 3, −4

More Math Vocab

Here are three more math vocab terms. Memorize them, practice using them, and remember to underline them in questions. That will avoid heaps of careless errors.

Factors—numbers that divide into a number evenly (i.e., without a remainder).

Example: The factors of 48 are 1, 2, 3, 4, 6, 8, 12, 16, 24, 48.

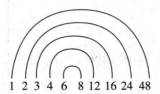

1 2 3 4 6 8 12 16 24 48

When asked for the factors of a number, make a list of pairs like the ones shown above. This eliminates the possibility of missing any.

Prime factors—the factors of a number that are also prime numbers. (Remember, a prime number is a number whose only factors are 1 and itself.)

Example: The prime factors of 48 are 2 and 3. These are the factors of 48 that also happen to be prime numbers.

Multiples—all the numbers that are divisible by a certain number.

Example: The multiples of 3 are 3, 6, 9, 12, 15, 18, 21, etc.

Now, let's take a look at the question from the Pretest.

9. If P is the set of all <u>different</u>, real number, prime factors of 100, how many members does set P contain?

(A) None   (B) 2   (C) 3   (D) 8

Solution: To complete this question, we factor 100 just as we factored 48 above.

Then we circle any prime numbers in the list. The numbers 2 and 5 are the only prime numbers in the list, so set P has two members.

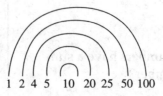

1 2 4 5 10 20 25 50 100

Correct answer: B

SAT Math Mantra #9
Anytime you see a math vocab term, underline it.

More Math Vocab Drills

Brian's Math Magic Tricks
Trick #1—Multiples
Answer the following questions aloud.

What is 2×2 ?
What is 4×2 ?
What is 8×2 ?
What is 16×2 ?
What is 32×2 ?
What is 64×2 ?
Name a vegetable.

Turn to the solutions page to be amazed.

Easy

1. Each of the following is a factor of 120 EXCEPT

   Ⓐ 7
   Ⓑ 6
   Ⓒ 5
   Ⓓ 4

2. Which of the following is an odd number that is a factor of 114 ?

   Ⓐ 2
   Ⓑ 13
   Ⓒ 55
   Ⓓ 57

3. How many integer factors does the number 48 have?

   Ⓐ None
   Ⓑ 3
   Ⓒ 8
   Ⓓ 10

Medium

4. If P is the set of all different, real number, prime factors of 48 that are also factors of 100, how many members does set P contain?

   Ⓐ None
   Ⓑ 1
   Ⓒ 2
   Ⓓ 3

5. What is the lowest number that is a multiple of 10, 12, and 15 ?

   Ⓐ 1800
   Ⓑ 900
   Ⓒ 120
   Ⓓ 60

Hard

6. If a, b, and c are different prime numbers, how many factors does ab^2c have?

   Ⓐ 3
   Ⓑ 9
   Ⓒ 12
   Ⓓ 15

Systems of Equations

There are several ways to solve a system of equations. In school you learned the linear combination and substitution methods, which we'll look at below and in the drill solutions. You can also graph the two equations to find the coordinate at which they intersect. Sometimes, you can even simply use the answers and test which answer choice works.

Sometimes the SAT might also ask about a system of inequalities. That just means you have to decide if each line is dotted or solid and whether you shade above or below the line. We'll go over this in the solution to question #6 in the drills.

Now, let's take a look at the question from the Pretest.

$$-2x = 8y + 6$$

$$-3(2y + 4) = 4x - 14$$

 10. What is the x-value of the solution (x, y) to the system of equations above?

Solution: The first step for a system of equations question is to ask yourself, "Self, which method is easiest for this question?" The best method will save you time and reduce the risk of a careless error. In this case, substitution is best. Divide the first equation by -2 to get:

$$\frac{-2x}{-2} = \frac{8y}{-2} + \frac{6}{-2}$$

$$x = -4x + -3$$

Now, plug $-4x + (-3)$ in for y in the second equation. Then solve for x:

$$-3(2(-4x - 3) + 4) = 4x - 14$$

$$-3((-8x - 6) + 4) = 4x - 14$$

$$-3(-8x - 2) = 4x - 14$$

$$24x + 6 = 4x - 14$$

$$20x = 8$$

$$x = \frac{8}{20} = \frac{2}{5} \text{ WHEW!}$$

Correct answer: $\frac{2}{5}$

SAT Math Mantra #10

To solve a system of equations, use substitution or linear combination.

Systems of Equations Drills

Medium

$3y = 12 + 6x$
$3x + 4y = 60$

1 What is the *x*-value of the solution to the system of equations above?

(A) 4

(B) 5

(C) 6

(D) 7

$2x + 3y = 12$
$3x - 3y = 8$

2 What is the *y*-value of the solution to the system of equations above?

(A) 4

(B) $\dfrac{4}{3}$

(C) $\dfrac{3}{4}$

(D) 1

$3y + 9x = 3$
$y + 3x = 1$

3 How many solutions (x, y) are there to the system of equations above?

(A) Zero

(B) One

(C) Two

(D) More than two

$3y - 2x = m$
$6y - nx = -5$

4 In the system of equations above, *m* and *n* are constants. If the system has no solutions, what is the value of *n*?

(A) 5

(B) 4

(C) 3

(D) 2

5 Jake and Sarah bake two types of desserts for the National Honor Society Fundraiser, chocolate chip cookies and crème brûlée. At the fundraiser, each chocolate chip cookie costs $1.50 and each serving of crème brûlée costs $4.50. If they sell a total of 50 desserts and raise $120, how many servings of crème brûlée did they sell?

(A) None

(B) 10

(C) 15

(D) 50

Hard

$2x + y > a$
$3x + y < b$

6 If $(0, 0)$ is a solution to the system of inequalities above, which of the following is true?

(A) $a = b$

(B) $a > b$

(C) $a < b$

(D) $2a = 3b$

Green Circle, Black Diamond: Slaloming Slope I

Slope questions appear on every SAT. This topic could fill a college-level course, but the SAT tests only a few concepts.

Most importantly, to find the slope of two ordered pairs, use the *slope formula:*

$$\text{Slope} = \frac{y_1 - y_2}{x_1 - x_2}$$

You should also know these other groovy SAT slope facts:

- The slope of a line measures its steepness—the steeper the line, the bigger the slope.
- A line has a positive slope if it rises from left to right.
- A line has a negative slope if it falls from left to right.
- A horizontal line has a slope of 0.

Let's apply this on the question from the Pretest.

11. If the slope of a line through the points (2, 4) and (0, b) is 1, what is the value of b?

(A) −2   (B) −1   (C) 1   (D) 2

Solution: Plug the two points into the slope equation.

$$\frac{y_1 - y_2}{x_1 - x_2} \Rightarrow \frac{4 - b}{2 - 0} \Rightarrow \frac{4 - b}{2} = 1$$

Once you have $\frac{4 - b}{2} = 1$, you can simply "Use the Answers" and try each answer choice to see which one makes the equation work. Skill Preview: As we will see in Skill 20, you could also cross-multiply to solve this equation.

Correct answer: D

SAT Math Mantra #11
**The slope of a line measures its steepness; the steeper the line,
the bigger the slope.**

Green Circle, Black Diamond: Slaloming Slope I Drills

Easy

1 If the slope of a line through the points $(3, a)$ and $(-2, -4)$ is $\frac{3}{5}$, what is the value of a ?

- (A) -2
- (B) -1
- (C) 0
- (D) 1

2 What is the slope of the line through the point $(2, -3)$ and the origin?

- (A) -2.5
- (B) -1.5
- (C) -1
- (D) 0.5

3 Which of the following is closest to the slope of the line in the figure below?

- (A) 0
- (B) $\frac{1}{4}$
- (C) $\frac{1}{2}$
- (D) 1

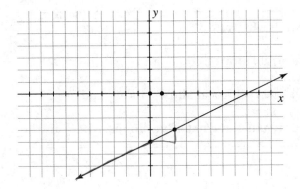

Medium

4 In the figure below, the line containing (a, b) passes through the origin. What is the value of $\frac{b}{a}$?

- (A) -1
- (B) 0
- (C) 1
- (D) 3

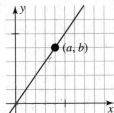

Hard

5 In the xy coordinate plane below, the indicated diameters of the two circles shown are parallel to the y-axis. If the points M and N are centers of the circles, what is the slope of line MN (not shown)?

- (A) $\frac{2}{3}$
- (B) $\frac{2}{5}$
- (C) $\frac{3}{5}$
- (D) 1

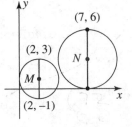

Green Circle, Black Diamond: Slaloming Slope II

Here are the rest of the slope rules on the SAT. You should memorize these; they are on **every** SAT!

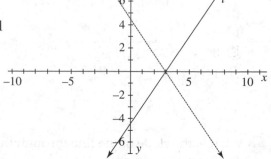

- Parallel lines have equal slopes.
- Perpendicular lines have negative reciprocal slopes. Example: $\frac{2}{3}$ and $-\frac{3}{2}$
- Lines reflected over the x-axis or y-axis have negative slopes. Example: $\frac{2}{3}$ and $-\frac{2}{3}$
  A reflection is like a mirror image. In the diagram to the right, line m is the reflection of line l over the x-axis.
- Skill 30 Preview: A line expressed in the form $y = ax + b$ has a slope of a. If the line is given in standard form $Ax + By = C$, use algebra to convert it to $y = ax + b$ form.

Let's take a look at the question from the Pretest.

12. In the xy coordinate plane, line j is the reflection of line k about the x-axis. If the slope of line j is $-\frac{3}{4}$, what is the slope of line k?

(A) $\frac{4}{3}$ (B) $\frac{3}{4}$ (C) $\frac{1}{4}$ (D) $-\frac{3}{4}$

Solution: This question is quite difficult for most students. But with our strategies it's very easy. We know that two lines that are reflections of each other simply have the same slope but with opposite signs; so instead of $-\frac{4}{3}$, line j has a slope of $+\frac{3}{4}$.

Correct answer: B

SAT Math Mantra # 12

Parallel lines have equal slopes, like $\frac{2}{3}$ and $\frac{2}{3}$.

Perpendicular lines have negative reciprocal slopes, like $\frac{2}{3}$ and $-\frac{3}{2}$.

And lines reflected over the x-axis or y-axis have negative slopes, like $\frac{2}{3}$ and $-\frac{2}{3}$.

Green Circle, Black Diamond: Slaloming Slope II Drills

Medium

1 What is the slope of the line perpendicular to the line through the points (2, 3) and (−1, 0) ?

Ⓐ −1

Ⓑ 0

Ⓒ 1

Ⓓ 3

2 If the line through the points (2, −3) and (4, p) is parallel to the line $y = -2x - 3$, what is the value of p ?

Ⓐ 7

Ⓑ 3

Ⓒ −3

Ⓓ −7

3 What is the slope of the line perpendicular to the line through the point (2, −3) and the origin?

Ⓐ 0.4

Ⓑ $\frac{2}{3}$

Ⓒ 1

Ⓓ −2

4 In the xy coordinate plane, line n is the reflection of line m about the x-axis. If the slope of line m is $\frac{2}{3}$, what is the slope of line n ?

Ⓐ 1

Ⓑ −1

Ⓒ $\frac{2}{3}$

Ⓓ $-\frac{2}{3}$

Hard

5 If the slope of a line through the points (2, 4) and (0, b) is 1, and the line through (b, 4) and (m, 6) is parallel to that line, what is the value of m ?

Ⓐ 0

Ⓑ 2

Ⓒ 4

Ⓓ 6

The Sports Page: Using Tables and Graphs

Tables and graphs display information, just like the sports page lists a team's wins and losses. In fact, using tables and graphs should feel no different than checking stats for your favorite Red Sox pitcher, Halo high scorer, or Guitar Hero hero.

SAT Math Mantra #13
The key to understanding tables and graphs is to read the headings
and the legend, if there is one.

The SAT uses six kinds of tables and graphs. Tables display information in rows and columns. Often the SAT asks you to use the last row or column, which shows totals. Pie graphs represent information as part of a pie. Line graphs display how data changes, often over time. Bar graphs compare the values of several items, such as sales of different toothpastes. Pictographs use small pictures to represent data. The key to pictographs lies in noticing the legend. If each icon represents 8 books, then half of an icon represents 4 books, not half of a book. Scatterplots compare two aspects of a group. When the SAT gives a scatterplot, it often asks you to name the equation of the line that best fits the data. Just sketch a line, estimate its y intercept and slope, and choose the equation (see Skill 30) that matches best.

Let's take a look at the question from the Pretest.

13. According to the graph on the right, which two SAT books sold the fewest copies?

(A) SAT Math and I♥SATs
(B) I♥SATs and Top 50 Skills
(C) I♥SATs and SAT Success
(D) SAT Success and SAT Math

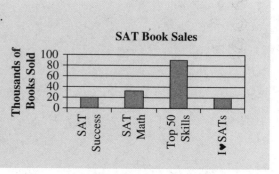

Solution: Obviously, Top 50 Skills is a stellar book and would sell the most, not the least copies, so that is out. According to the graph, SAT Success and I♥SATs sold the fewest copies.

Correct answer: C

The Sports Page: Using Tables and Graphs Drills

Easy

	Rookies	Veterans	Total
Yankees	*a*	*b*	*c*
Red Sox	*d*	*e*	*f*
Total	*g*	*h*	*i*

1 In the table above, each letter represents the number of home runs for that category. Which of the following must be equal to *i* ?

  I. $c + f$
 II. $a + b + d + e$
III. $g + c$

Ⓐ I only
Ⓑ II only
Ⓒ I and II
Ⓓ II and III

Medium

Favorite Class Survey

2 The chart above shows the answers 500 people students gave when asked to name their favorite teacher. Sra. Moran and Ms. Nicholas received the most votes. According to the graph, how many total votes were cast for these two teachers?

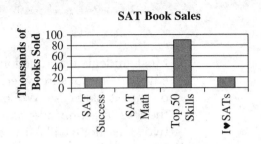

3 According to the graph above, the four books averaged sales closest to

Ⓐ 22
Ⓑ 41
Ⓒ 22,000
Ⓓ 41,000

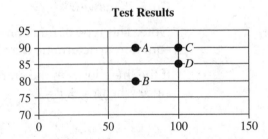

4 The grid above shows the grades on two tests for students in Mr. Okin's history class. The *x*-axis represents results on test I, and the *y*-axis represents results on test II. Which student improved the most from test I to test II?

Ⓐ A
Ⓑ B
Ⓒ C
Ⓓ D

Function Questions on the SAT, Type I

Most students fear functions. "I suck at functions," I hear from almost every new student. I'm not sure where this attitude comes from, but here's the good news: functions on the SAT are easy. While functions could be the topic of a full-year university course, the SAT tests only a few kinds of function questions. If you feared functions, the next two skills alone will earn you three more correct questions and raise your score 20 to 30 points!

Functions are just a type of equation, like $y = mx + b$. To show that an equation is a function, sometimes people replace the y with $f(x)$ or $g(x)$ or $h(x)$. That's it. Easy. To solve functions, remember that $f(x)$ is just a fancy way of saying y. So $f(x) = 2x - 1$ means the same as $y = 2x - 1$.

Now, let's look at the question from the Pretest.

14. If $f(x) = 2x + 1$, what is $f(3)$?

Solution: This is the first type of function question. This type simply asks you to plug the 3 in for x in the equation or graph. Cake! So $f(3) = 2(3) + 1 = 7$.

Correct answer: 7

Note: This type of function question might also ask you to use a graph instead of an equation to determine the answer. For example:

If the line shown in the graph below is $y = f(x)$, find $f(3)$. Based on the graph, $f(3) = 7$, since when $x = 3$, $y = 7$.

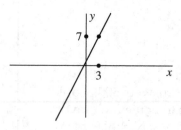

SAT Math Mantra #14
$f(3)$ means "plug 3 in for x."

Function Questions on the SAT, Type I Drills

Easy

1 If $f(x) = 2x^3 - 2$, what is the value of $f(-2)$?

Ⓐ −18
Ⓑ −16
Ⓒ −10
Ⓓ 8

Medium

2 For which of the following functions is $f(5) < f(-5)$?

Ⓐ $f(x) = 2x^2$
Ⓑ $f(x) = 2$
Ⓒ $f(x) = \dfrac{2}{x}$
Ⓓ $f(x) = 2 - x^3$

x	f(x)
0	−1
1	2
2	11
3	26

3 The table above shows the values of the quadratic function f for selected values of x. Which of the following defines f ?

Ⓐ $f(x) = x^2 + 1$
Ⓑ $f(x) = x^2 + 2$
Ⓒ $f(x) = 3x^2 - 2$
Ⓓ $f(x) = 3x^2 - 1$

4 The total weekly soap use, in pints, from washing x cars is given by the function $g(x) = 5x - (4x + k)$, where k is a constant. If last week 140 cars were washed, using 3 pints of soap, what is the value of k?

Ⓐ −137
Ⓑ −31
Ⓒ 1
Ⓓ 137

5 If $m(n) = n^2 + 2n$ and $h(n) = 2n^2 - n$, then $m(h(3)) =$

Ⓐ 15
Ⓑ 255
Ⓒ 315
Ⓓ 435

6 If $f(x) = 2x + 3$ and $g(x) = f(x) + 2$, $g(2) =$

Ⓐ 4
Ⓑ 7
Ⓒ 9
Ⓓ 13

Hard

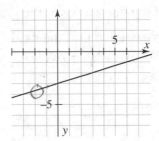

7 The graph of $y = f(x)$ is shown above. If $f(3) = m$, which of the following could be the value of $f(m)$?

Ⓐ $\dfrac{3}{5}$
Ⓑ 3
Ⓒ $-\dfrac{11}{3}$
Ⓓ −7

Function Questions on the SAT, Type II

Repeat after me, "I do not fear functions. I enjoy them. They are fun, easy, and interesting." As long as you don't get intimidated when you see the $f(x)$, functions are easy!

SAT Math Mantra #15

$f(m) = 9$ means "What did we plug into the equation for x to get a result of 9 ?"

Let's look at the question from the Pretest.

15. If $f(x) = 2x + 1$ and $f(m) = 9$, what is m ?

Solution: This is the second type of function question. It asks, "What did we plug into the equation for x to get a result of 9?" To solve, plug m in for x to get a result of 9, and solve for m:

$$9 = 2m + 1 \qquad \text{subtract 1 from both sides}$$
$$\underline{-1 \qquad\quad -1}$$
$$\frac{8}{2} = \frac{2m}{2} \qquad \text{divide by 2}$$
$$\boxed{4 = m}$$

Correct answer: 4

Note: This type of function question might also ask you to use a graph instead of an equation to determine the answer. For example:

If the line shown in the graph below is $y = f(x)$, and if $f(p) = 9$, find p.

We need to find the x value on the graph below that corresponds to a y value of 9. An x value of 4 yields a y value of 9.

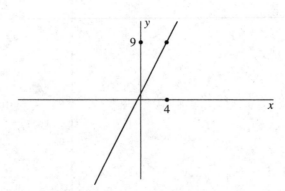

Function Questions on the SAT, Type II Drills

Medium

1 If $f(x) = 2x^2 - 3$, and $f(m) = -3$, what is the value of m ?

(A) -3

(B) -2

(C) 0

(D) 2

2 Let the function g be defined by $g(t) = 3(t^3 - 5)$. When $g(a) = -39$, what is the value of $4 - 2a$?

(A) -31

(B) -13

(C) -8

(D) 8

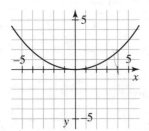

3 The graph of $y = f(x)$ is shown above. If $f(p) = 2$, which of the following is a possible value of p ?

(A) -5

(B) -4

(C) 0

(D) 2

Hard

4 If $m(n) = n^2 + n$ and $h(n) = n^2 - n$, which of the following is equivalent to $m(p - 1)$?

(A) $h(p)$

(B) $h(p) - 1$

(C) $h(p) - 2$

(D) $h(p) + 1$

5 Let the function h be defined by $h(x) = x - 2$. If $3h(v) = 54$, what is the value of $h(2v)$?

6 Let the function g be defined by $g(t) = t^2 - 3$. If m is a real number, how many possible values will make $g(3m) = 3g(m)$?

Make It Real

This is my single favorite SAT strategy. You're asking yourself, "What kind of dork has a favorite SAT strategy?" I do. Anyway, this strategy is amazing.

Let's take a look at the question from the Pretest.

16. Grandma Jones is making cookies for the fair. She needs x cups of flour per batch. Each batch makes c number of cookies. If she has 10 cups of flour, in terms of x and c, how many cookies can she make?

(A) xc (B) $10xc$ (C) $\dfrac{10c}{x}$ (D) $\dfrac{10x}{c}$

Solution: You'd have to be Einstein to get this question; it's too theoretical. So we take it out of theory and "Make It Real." We choose real numbers in place of the variables, and it becomes totally easy. We can choose any numbers that seem to fit the equation, and we might as well choose numbers that work evenly and avoid decimals. For example,

- Let's say she needs 2 cups of flour per batch, so $x = 2$.
- Therefore, since she has 10 cups of flour, she can make 5 batches.
- Each batch produces c cookies. Let's say $c = 20$, so she can make 5 batches of 20 cookies. She can therefore make 100 cookies. EASY!

Now, we just go through the answer choices and plug our values for x and c into each. Whichever choice yields an answer of 100 is correct! So the answer is C, since

$$\frac{(10)(c)}{x} = \frac{(10)(20)}{2} = 100.$$

Correct answer: C

This strategy turns very difficult questions into much easier ones!

SAT Math Mantra #16
When you see <u>variables</u> in the question and <u>variables</u> in the answer choices, especially for word problems, use "Make It Real."

Remember to try all answer choices. If more than one choice works for the values you choose, try a second set of values as a tie breaker.

Make It Real Drills

Easy

1 If p represents an even integer, which of the following expressions also represents an even integer?

(A) $p - 3$

(B) $2p - 1$

(C) $2p - 2$

(D) $3p + 1$

Medium

2 If x days ago Striped caterpillar was born and she is now n days older than her friend Yellow caterpillar, how old is Yellow in terms of x and n ?

(A) n

(B) $x - n$

(C) $n - x$

(D) nx

3 If p is a negative number, then $(5 \times 10^p) + (1 \times 10^p) =$

(A) $\dfrac{5}{10}$

(B) $\dfrac{6}{10^{2p}}$

(C) $6(10)^p$

(D) $\dfrac{6}{10^p}$

4 A number q is multiplied by 7. The result is then added to 7. This result is then divided by 7. Which of the following expresses, in terms of q, the final result?

(A) q

(B) $q + 14$

(C) $7q - 7$

(D) $q + 1$

Hard

5 If $-2 \le m \le 5$ and $-1 \le n \le 2$, what are all possible values of mn ?

(A) $mn = 4$

(B) $2 \le mn \le 4$

(C) $-2 \le mn \le 10$

(D) $-5 \le mn \le 10$

6 If $-1 < n < 0$, which of the following expresses the correct ordering of n, n^2, and n^3 ?

(A) $n < n^2 < n^3$

(B) $n^2 < n < n^3$

(C) $n < n^3 < n^2$

(D) $n^3 < n < n^2$

7 If $m = \dfrac{3a^2}{v}$, what happens to the value of m when a and v are both doubled?

(A) m is doubled

(B) m is halved

(C) m does not change

(D) m is multiplied by 4

Perimeter, Area, Volume

Every formula that you need to solve for area or volume in an SAT question is shown in the information box at the beginning of each math section. The box tells you:

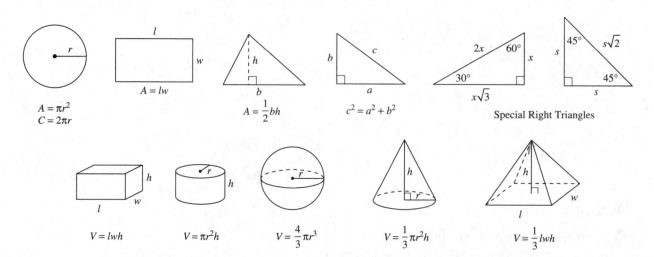

$A = \pi r^2$
$C = 2\pi r$

$A = lw$

$A = \frac{1}{2}bh$

$c^2 = a^2 + b^2$

Special Right Triangles

$V = lwh$

$V = \pi r^2 h$

$V = \frac{4}{3}\pi r^3$

$V = \frac{1}{3}\pi r^2 h$

$V = \frac{1}{3}lwh$

For area and volume on the SAT, these are all the formulas that you'll need. Now, let's practice using them.

SAT Math Mantra #17
The SAT only expects you to use formulas provided in the question or in the info box at the beginning of the section.

Let's take a look at the question from the Pretest.

17. In the figure to the right, the perimeter of square *BCDF* is 12 and the perimeter of rectangle *ACEG* is 30. If *AB* and *DE* are each positive integers, what is one possible value of the area of rectangle *ACEG* ?

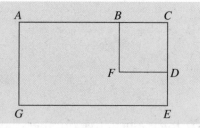

Solution: Since the perimeter of square *BCDF* is 12, each side must be 12 ÷ 4 = 3; and since the perimeter of rectangle *ACEG* is 30, *AB* + *DE* = 15 − 3 − 3 = 9. So *AB* and *DE* can be any two integers that add up to 9, for example, 1 and 8; and *AC* and *CE* would each be 3 units longer, 4 and 11. There are four such possibilities for the area of *ACEG*:

$4 \times 11 = 44, 5 \times 10 = 50, 6 \times 9 = 54, 7 \times 8 = 56$. Any one of these is a correct answer.

Correct answers: 44, 50, 54, or 56

Perimeter, Area, Volume Drills

Easy

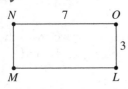
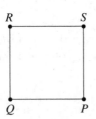

1 If the square and the rectangle above have equal perimeters, what is the length of $\overline{RS}$?

Ⓐ 5

Ⓑ 6

Ⓒ 8

Ⓓ 10

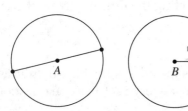

Note: Figure not drawn to scale.

2 For the circles above, the diameter of circle A is 10, and the radius of circle B is half the diameter of circle A. What is the area of circle B?

Ⓐ 5

Ⓑ 25π

Ⓒ 100π

Ⓓ π

Medium

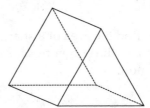

3 The three-dimensional figure pictured above has square and triangular faces. If each square face has area m and each triangular face has area n, what is the total surface area of the figure in terms of m and n?

Ⓐ $m+n$

Ⓑ $2(m+n)$

Ⓒ $3m+2n$

Ⓓ $3m+3n$

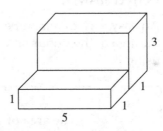

4 The figure above shows the dimensions of a children's stacking block that is composed of rectangular solids. What is the volume of the block?

Ⓐ 3

Ⓑ 5

Ⓒ 20

Ⓓ 30

To find the area of a shaded region, just subtract the area of the smaller figure from the area of the bigger figure. You might also be asked to find the perimeter of a shaded region.

Let's look at the question from the Pretest.

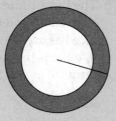

18. In the diagram above, if the area of the large circle is 10 and the area of the small circle is 8, what is the area of the shaded region?

Solution: The area of a shaded region is found by subtracting the little guy from the big guy. So $10 - 8 = 2$ and 2 is the area of the shaded region.

Correct answer: 2

An easy way to remember it: "The area of a donut equals the area of the big guy minus the area of the donut hole." This is a great formula. Almost every SAT has one question using it.

SAT Math Mantra #18
The area of a donut equals the area of the big guy minus the area of the donut hole.

Donuts Drills

Medium

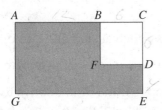

1 In the figure above, the perimeter of square *BCDF* is 24, *DE* = 4, and *AB* = 12. What is the area of the shaded region?

- Ⓐ 204
- Ⓑ 180
- Ⓒ 144
- Ⓓ 36

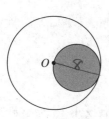

2 The small circle above is tangent to the large circle. If the radius of the large circle is 8, what is the area of the unshaded region?

- Ⓐ 48π
- Ⓑ 45π
- Ⓒ 32π
- Ⓓ 16π

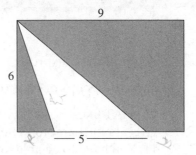

3 In the figure above, what is the area of the shaded region?

Hard

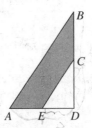

4 In the figure above, triangles *ADB* and *EDC* are similar. If *AD* = 4, *ED* = 2, and *BD* = 6, what is the area of the shaded region?

Baking Granola Bars . . . Ratios

A ratio simply expresses a relationship between two numbers, such as: to bake granola bars, use 7 cups of oats to 2 cups of sugar. This can be written as $7 : 2$ or $\frac{7}{2}$ or even 7 to 2.

The SAT likes to see if you can play with the ratios. For example, if the ratio of boys to girls at Northampton High School is 5 to 6, then the ratio of girls to total students is 6 to 11. You have to be able to move between parts and the whole. Also remember that the numbers in a ratio may be reduced versions of the actual numbers. For example, if the ratio of boys to girls in a certain class is $\frac{2}{3}$, there might not actually be 2 boys and 3 girls, there might really be 4 boys and 6 girls. In this example $\frac{2}{3}$ is the reduced version and not the actual numbers: $\frac{2}{3} = \frac{4}{6}$.

SAT Math Mantra #19
4 boys to 5 girls could also be expressed 5 girls to 9 students.
Also a ratio can be a reduced version of the real numbers.

Let's look at the question from the Pretest.

19. In a mixture of pretzels and corn chips, the ratio of pretzels to corn chips is 3 to 7. How many pretzels will be in a mixture that has 100 total pieces?

(A) 70   (B) 50   (C) 37   (D) 30

Solution: This is a classic ratio question. You are given the ratio of pretzels to corn chips but are asked for the ratio of pretzels to total mixture. So switch the ratio. There are 3 pretzels per 7 corn chips, so there are 3 pretzels per 10 pieces total (3 pretzels + 7 corn chips = 10 delicious munchables). Now, just try the answers to see which one gives a ratio with 100 that is equal to $3 : 10$. Choice D is correct since $30 : 100$ equals $3 : 10$. You could also solve this question by setting up a proportion and cross-multiplying, which we will discuss in the next Skill.

Correct answer: D

Baking Granola Bars . . . Ratios Drills

Easy

1 In a basket of whole vegetables, the ratio of carrots to potatoes is 2 to 7. Which of the following could NOT be the number of carrots in the basket?

Ⓐ 2
Ⓑ 3
Ⓒ 4
Ⓓ 10

2 In a basket of apples and pears, 2 out of every 5 pieces of fruit are pears. Which of the following could be the number of apples in the basket?

Ⓐ 7
Ⓑ 14
Ⓒ 15
Ⓓ 22

3 A 60-question test included 20 true/false questions. What fraction of the test was not true/false?

Medium

4 If the degree measures of the three angles in a triangle are in the ratio 1 : 3 : 5, what is the measure of the smallest angle?

Ⓐ 5°
Ⓑ 10°
Ⓒ 15°
Ⓓ 20°

5 If the degree measures of the three angles in a triangle are in the ratio 1 : 3 : 5, what is the difference between the measures of the largest and the smallest angles?

Ⓐ 70°
Ⓑ 80°
Ⓒ 90°
Ⓓ 100°

6 In a mixture of pretzels and corn chips, the ratio of pretzels to corn chips is 3 ounces of pretzels to 7 ounces of corn chips. How many ounces of pretzels will be in 16 ounces of the mixture?

More Granola Bars . . . Proportions and Cross-Multiplying

Two ratios that are equal are called a proportion. For example, $\frac{5}{12} = \frac{10}{24}$ is a proportion. If one of the four numbers in that proportion is unknown, cross-multiply to solve for it. For example, if $\frac{5}{12} = \frac{x}{40}$ and we want to find the value of x, just cross-multiply: $(5)(40) = (12)x$. Then use algebra to solve for x (divide both sides by 12 to get $x = 16.66$). Anytime the SAT shows you a proportion, they want you to cross-multiply. This is an exciting strategy. When you come to a proportion on the SAT, with our mantra, you will **always** get it right!

SAT Math Mantra #20
When you see a proportion on the SAT, cross-multiply.

Let's look at the question from the Pretest.

20. If the numerator of a fraction is 3 more than the denominator, and the fraction equals $\frac{4}{3}$, what is the numerator of the fraction?

    (A) 3   (B) 6   (C) 9   (D) 12

Solution: "Numerator" is just a super fancy word for the top of a fraction, and "denominator" is just the bottom. So if the numerator is 3 more than the denominator and the fraction equals $\frac{4}{3}$, we can represent this proportion as $\frac{d+3}{d} = \frac{4}{3}$ and cross-multiply to solve for d. $(d + 3)(3) = (d)(4)$, which equals $3d + 9 = 4d$. Collect like terms and $d = 9$. Notice that the question does not ask for d, but for the numerator, which is $d + 3$, so the numerator is 12. Always check to make sure that you've answered the question and didn't stop in a preliminary step. Skill 42 Preview: Stopping too early is the most common SAT careless error that other students make.

Correct answer: D

More Granola Bars . . . Proportions and Cross-Multiplying Drills

Easy

1 According to Grandma Clara's recipe, 15 pounds of spelt flour is needed to make 50 cakes of dafillin. At this rate, how many pounds of flour is needed to make 1 cake?

(A) 0.1

(B) 0.2

(C) 0.3

(D) 1

2 If $\dfrac{m}{12} = \dfrac{5}{n}$ what is the value of mn ?

(A) 60

(B) 40

(C) 30

(D) 20

3 If $\dfrac{m}{12} = \dfrac{3m}{n}$, what is the value of n ?

(A) 2.25

(B) 9

(C) 18

(D) 36

Medium

4 In a certain model airplane $\dfrac{1}{4}$ inch represents 4 feet. If the wing on the model is 1.5 inches, how long, in feet, is the wing on the actual plane?

(A) $\dfrac{4}{5}$

(B) 1

(C) 18

(D) 24

Hard

5 If m, n, o, and p are all positive integers, all the following can be equivalent to each other EXCEPT

(A) $\dfrac{m}{n} = \dfrac{o}{p}$

(B) $\dfrac{mp}{on} = 1$

(C) $\dfrac{p}{n} = \dfrac{o}{m}$

(D) $\dfrac{m}{p} = \dfrac{o}{n}$

Use the Diagram

Figures on the SAT are drawn perfectly to scale. I think they use lasers and fancy space-age machines to draw them—they're very accurate. Since they are so accurate, we can use the diagrams to estimate the answer to many questions. For a year in geometry class you were taught not to do this, and on the SAT it makes the question so much easier that it feels "cheap," like you are cheating. It's not! It's actually what they want you to do. Remember the test is supposed to test your cleverness, not just what you learned in math class. This strategy brings out your innate cleverness.

Often in "Use the Diagram" we are given the length of some part of the diagram, and we use that to estimate the unknown. We've all done this before. Imagine you are on a road trip driving in a car. You look at the map and say, "We have to go from here to there on this squiggly highway." The map key says that each inch is 100 miles, so you use your thumb to represent an inch and you estimate the length of the squiggly line highway. That's the "Use the Diagram" strategy!

Sometimes "Use the Diagram" gives you the exact correct answer; at other times it is only a Plan B for when you can't figure out which of our geometry strategies to use.

Let's use this strategy on the question from the Pretest.

21. In the figure below, *ABED* is a square with sides of length 6. If *EC* = 3, what is the perimeter of quadrilateral *ABCD* ?

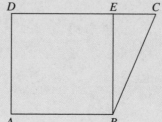

(A) 24

(B) 27

(C) $18 + 3\sqrt{5}$

(D) $21 + 3\sqrt{5}$

Solution: *AB*, *AD*, and *DE* are 6 and *EC* is 3, so we have a perimeter of at least 21 so far. We can use the Pythagorean theorem to get *BC*. We can also "Use the Diagram." Clearly *CB* is slightly longer than *EB*, so slightly longer than 6, let's say 6.5. Thus, the perimeter is approximately $6 + 6 + 6 + 3 + 6.5 \approx 27.5$. Now try the answers. Use your calculator to translate $3\sqrt{5}$ into a decimal — $3\sqrt{5} = 6.6$ — and see which answer matches. Choice D is correct.

Correct answer: D

SAT Math Mantra #21
"Use the Diagram" to estimate an answer.
Translate into decimals any answer choices that contain $\sqrt{\ }$ or π.

Use the Diagram Drills

Easy

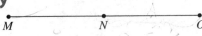

1 In the figure above, $MO = 12$ and $MN = NO$. Point A (not shown) is on the line between N and O such that $NA = AO$. What does MA equal?

Ⓐ 6
Ⓑ 9
Ⓒ 12
Ⓓ 15

Medium

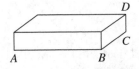

2 The rectangular solid above has edges of length 10, 4, and 2. If point M (not shown) is the midpoint of segment AB, what is the length of MC?

Ⓐ $\sqrt{17}$
Ⓑ $\sqrt{26}$
Ⓒ $\sqrt{35}$
Ⓓ $\sqrt{41}$

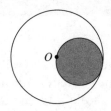

3 The small circle above is tangent to the large circle. If the radius of the large circle is 6, what is the perimeter of the unshaded region?

Ⓐ 18π
Ⓑ 15π
Ⓒ 12π
Ⓓ 8π

Hard

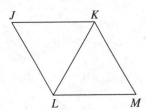

4 In the figure above, the measures of all five line segments are equal. What is the ratio of the length of $\overline{LK}$ to the length of $\overline{JM}$ (not shown)?

Ⓐ $\dfrac{\sqrt{3}}{3}$

Ⓑ $\dfrac{\sqrt{6}}{3}$

Ⓒ $\sqrt{2}$

Ⓓ $\dfrac{3\sqrt{3}}{3}$

Art Class

Here's your chance to relive your sixth-grade art class memories. We love the "Use the Diagram" strategy, but can we use it for diagrams that specifically say, "Note: Figure not drawn to scale"? What are we to do? Are we lost? NO! These questions are even easier. Simply resketch the picture somewhat accurately and then "Use the Diagram." It turns out that often the whole question is hinged on it being out of scale; when you put it into scale, the answer becomes obvious.

Also, while we're in art class here's another great strategy. If a question describes a diagram, but none is shown, draw one. Sometimes this gives the answer immediately, and other times it shows you what to do next, but either way it always helps!

SAT Math Mantra #22
When a diagram is not drawn to scale, redraw it.
And when a picture is described but not shown, draw it!

Let's look at the Pretest question.

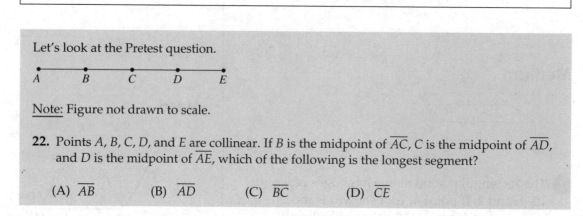

Note: Figure not drawn to scale.

22. Points A, B, C, D, and E are collinear. If B is the midpoint of $\overline{AC}$, C is the midpoint of $\overline{AD}$, and D is the midpoint of $\overline{AE}$, which of the following is the longest segment?

   (A) $\overline{AB}$ (B) $\overline{AD}$ (C) $\overline{BC}$ (D) $\overline{CE}$

Solution: Simply redraw the diagram to scale, following the instructions in the question:

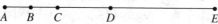

Then the answer is obvious. Of the choices, $\overline{CE}$ is longest.

Correct answer: D

Art Class Drills

Easy

1 If points *L*, *M*, *N*, and *O* are collinear, *LM* = *MO* = 12, and *N* is between *M* and *O*, which of the following could be the measure of segment *LN* ?

Ⓐ 4
Ⓑ 8
Ⓒ 12
Ⓓ 15

Medium

2 In an *xy* coordinate plane (not shown) three points *Q*, *R*, and *S* have coordinates (2, 7), (2, 3), and (5, *b*), respectively. If the three points determine a right triangle, what is one possible value of *b* ?

3 If the sides of quadrilateral *ACEG* below are all equal, and ∠*AGE* = 90°, what is the ratio of *AE* to *CE* ?

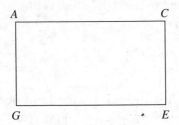

Note: Figure not drawn to scale.

Ⓐ 3 to 1
Ⓑ 2 to 1
Ⓒ $\sqrt{2}$ to 1
Ⓓ $\sqrt{2}$ to 2

4 A cube has edges of length 2. If point *M* is the midpoint of edge *AB*, what is the length of the segment from point *M* to the center of the cube?

Ⓐ $\sqrt{2}$
Ⓑ $\sqrt{3}$
Ⓒ $2\sqrt{2}$
Ⓓ $2\sqrt{3}$

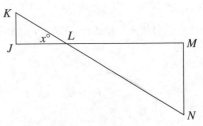

Note: Figure not drawn to scale.

5 In the figure above, segments *MN* and *JK* are each perpendicular to *JM*. If *x* = 30, the measure of *LN* is 12, and the measure of *KL* is 4, what is the measure of *JM* ?

Ⓐ $3\sqrt{3}$ (approximately 5.19)
Ⓑ $5\sqrt{3}$ (approximately 8.66)
Ⓒ $8\sqrt{3}$ (approximately 12.12)
Ⓓ $10\sqrt{3}$ (approximately 13.86)

The Six-Minute Abs of Geometry: Length of a Side I

In Skills 4–7, we looked at finding missing angles in a diagram. Skills 23–25 show you how to find a missing side in a diagram. **You do not need to memorize these formulas; they are provided in the information box at the beginning of every math section.**

I come from a long line of teachers. My grandfather, Herman, was a beloved teacher and principal in Zshmolphf, Austria (mostly true). His father was a scholar (true). His father's father was a scholar. Some say we can trace our lineage back thousands of years to the James Brown of geometry, the godfather of good math, your friend and mine, the mighty Pythagoras (lie), best known for his theorem $a^2 + b^2 = c^2$. Pythagoras is also definitely a favorite of the folks at the SAT. His theorem is used on EVERY SAT.

Use the Pythagorean theorem, $a^2 + b^2 = c^2$, to find the length of a side of a right triangle when you are given the lengths of the other two. As I said, this is used on EVERY SAT. In fact, anytime you see a right triangle on the SAT, you will probably need it. Just fill the two sides that you know into the equation, and solve for the third. Here's an example:

If $a = 6$ and $c = 10$, what is the value of b ?

$$a^2 + b^2 = c^2$$
$$6^2 + b^2 = 10^2$$
$$36 + b^2 = 100$$
$$b^2 = 64$$
$$b = 8$$

SAT Math Mantra #23
When you see a right triangle, try $a^2 + b^2 = c^2$.

Let's use good ol' Pythagoras on the question from the Pretest.

23. In right triangle ABC (not shown), the measure of AB is 6 and the measure of BC is 10. Which of the following could be the measure of AC ?

   (A) 3   (B) 4   (C) 6   (D) 8

Solution: Great review of SAT Math Mantra #22, "When a picture is described but not shown, draw it." This helps you visualize and organize the info and shows you what to do next. The question does not state whether 10 is another short side like 6 or whether it is the longest side. But we can "Use the Answers" and simply try each answer choice in $a^2 + b^2 = c^2$, always using the biggest number for c. Choice A is not correct since $3^2 + 6^2 \neq 10^2$, and choice B is not correct since $4^2 + 6^2 \neq 10^2$, and so on. Choice D is correct since $6^2 + 8^2 = 10^2$.

Correct answer: D

Easy

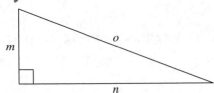

1 In the right triangle above, if $m = 5$ and $n = 12$, find the value of o.

Ⓐ 5
Ⓑ 12
Ⓒ 13
Ⓓ 15

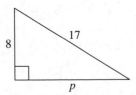

Note: Figure not drawn to scale.

2 If the figure above is a right triangle, what is the value of p?

Medium

3 In right triangle ABC (not shown), the measure of AB is 4 and the measure of BC is 10. Which of the following could be the measure of AC?

Ⓐ $2\sqrt{19}$
Ⓑ $2\sqrt{21}$
Ⓒ $2\sqrt{25}$
Ⓓ 84

Hard

4 In an xy coordinate plane (not shown), three points Q, R, and S have coordinates $(2, 3)$, $(7, 3)$, and $(2, m)$, respectively. If the three points determine a right triangle, with a hypotenuse of 13, and m is a positive integer, what is the value of m?

5 The lengths of the sides of a right triangle are consecutive integers, and the length of the longest side is x. Which of the following could be used to solve for x?

Ⓐ $(x - 2)^2 + (x - 1)^2 = x^2$
Ⓑ $x + x - 3 = x$
Ⓒ $(x - 2)(x - 1) = x^2$
Ⓓ $(x - 2) - (x - 1) = x$

The Six-Minute Abs of Geometry: Length of a Side II

When the Pythagorean theorem is not enough to find the length of a missing side, use one or both of the two "special right triangles."

① When the three angles of a triangle measure 30°, 60°, 90°, then the sides are x, $x\sqrt{3}$, and $2x$.

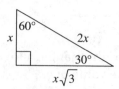

② When the three angles measure 45°, 45°, 90° (also called an isosceles right triangle), then the two short sides are equal, let's call them x, and the longest side measures $x\sqrt{2}$. Or, if you are given the long side, then the two short sides each measure $\dfrac{x}{\sqrt{2}}$.

SAT Math Mantra #24
When you see a 30°, 45°, or 60° angle in a right triangle, try using the special right triangles.

Now, let's use these on the question from the Pretest.

24. If triangle MNO (not shown) is congruent to triangle PQR shown below, which of the following is the measure of longest side of triangle MNO?

(A) 3
(B) $3\sqrt{3}$
(C) 6
(D) $6\sqrt{3}$

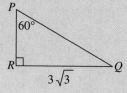

Solution: When you see a right triangle on the SAT, first try the Pythagorean theorem. Given only one side of the triangle, we don't have much info to use in the Pythagorean theorem, so try the special right triangles. **Also the 60° angle is a clue to use special right triangles. When you see a 60° angle, try special right triangles.** Since there is a 90° and a 60° angle, the third angle must be 30°, so it is a 30, 60, 90 triangle and follows the pattern x, $x\sqrt{3}$, and $2x$ for the three sides. (You do not need to memorize these; they are provided in the information box at the beginning at of every math section.) Therefore, $PR = 3$ and the longest side of PQR equals 6. Since the two triangles are congruent, the measure of the longest side of MNO must also be 6.

Correct answer: C

Medium

 1 In right triangle *MNO* (not shown), the measure of *MN* is 8 and the measure of *NO* is 4. Which of the following could be the measure of *OM* ?

   I. 4

   II. $4\sqrt{3}$

   III. 2

Ⓐ II only

Ⓑ III only

Ⓒ I and II

Ⓓ II and III

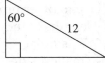

Note: Figure not drawn to scale.

2 What is the length of the shortest leg of a triangle congruent to the triangle shown above?

Ⓐ 3

Ⓑ $3\sqrt{3}$

Ⓒ 6

Ⓓ $3\sqrt{3}$

Hard

3 In an isosceles right triangle, the sum of measures of the two equal sides is 6. What is the measure of the longest side?

Ⓐ 3

Ⓑ $3\sqrt{2}$ (approximately 4.24)

Ⓒ 6

Ⓓ $3\sqrt{3}$ (approximately 5.19)

(Question 4 is very similar to a question you've seen before. See if you can solve it this time using special right triangles.)

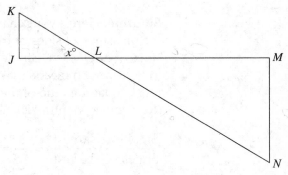

Note: Figure not drawn to scale.

4 In the figure above, segments *MN* and *JK* are each perpendicular to *JM*. If *x* = 30, the measure of *LN* is 10, and the measure of *KL* is 6, what is the measure of *JM* ?

Ⓐ $3\sqrt{3}$ (approximately 5.19)

Ⓑ $5\sqrt{3}$ (approximately 8.66)

Ⓒ $6\sqrt{3}$ (approximately 10.39)

Ⓓ $8\sqrt{3}$ (approximately 12.12)

The Six-Minute Abs of Geometry: Length of a Side III

I shall call him . . . Mini-Me.

Dr. Evil, *Austin Powers: The Spy Who Shagged Me* (New Line Cinema, 1999)

Similar triangles are two triangles where one is a shrinky version of the other, like Dr. Evil and Mini-Me. Since one is a shrunken version of the other, all sides are proportional.

Let's have a look at the question from the Pretest.

25. If triangle *MNO* (not shown) is similar to triangle *PQR* shown below and has a shortest side with length 4.5, which of the following could be the measure of the longest side of triangle *MNO* ?

(A) 4.5

(B) 6.5

(C) 9

(D) 12

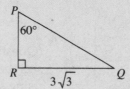

Solution: Here's your chance to see if you really learned Skill 24. We have to determine the measures of sides of triangle *PQR* shown above. Once you have the lengths of the sides of $\triangle PQR$, you can determine the lengths of $\triangle MNO$. Triangle *MNO* is "similar" to *PQR*, which means that the sides are proportional. So the ratio of the smallest sides must equal the ratio of the largest sides. Fill in the numbers and cross-multiply to solve. (Remember Mantra #20, "When you see a proportion, cross-multiply.")

$$\frac{\text{Smallest}}{\text{Smallest}} = \frac{\text{largest}}{\text{largest}} \Rightarrow \frac{3}{4.5} = \frac{6}{x}$$

So $3x = 27$ and $x = 9$.

Correct answer: C

SAT Math Mantra #25
Similar triangles have sides that are proportional.

Medium

1 Isosceles triangle ABC is similar to triangle MNO above. If $AC = 3$, $AB = 4$, and $NO = 6$, what is the measure of MO ?

Ⓐ 3

Ⓑ 4.5

Ⓒ 6

Ⓓ 7.5

3 The triangle pictured above is similar to triangle PRQ (not shown). If the ratio of the shortest side of the pictured triangle to the shortest side in triangle PQR is 2, what is the perimeter of triangle PQR ?

Ⓐ 1.5

Ⓑ 4

Ⓒ 5

Ⓓ 6

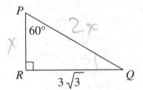

2 If triangle MNO (not shown) is similar to triangle PQR shown above, which of the following could be the measures of the three sides of triangle MNO ?

Ⓐ $3\sqrt{3}, 6\sqrt{3}, 9$

Ⓑ $6, 6\sqrt{3}, 12$

Ⓒ $6, 6, 12$

Ⓓ $3\sqrt{3}, 6\sqrt{3}, 6$

4 The lengths of the sides of two similar triangles (not shown) have a ratio of 3 : 5. The lengths of the larger triangle are 4, 5, and 6. If x represents the measure of the shortest side of the smaller triangle, which of the following could be used to find x ?

Ⓐ $\dfrac{3}{5} = \dfrac{x}{4}$

Ⓑ $\dfrac{3}{5} = \dfrac{4}{x}$

Ⓒ $\dfrac{3}{4} = \dfrac{4}{x}$

Ⓓ $\dfrac{3}{4} = \dfrac{x}{5}$

Nina the Ninja, Let's Get Zen! A Yoga Posture for the SAT

The SAT is a marathon, and you must pace yourself and manage your energy. It serves you to focus and try your absolute hardest. It does not serve you to tense your face as you work, to clench your butt, or to shake your foot. You can focus and give your all without getting an ulcer, and best of all, you can spend less energy and do better on the test. You can be like a warrior, a ninja, a Jedi.

Here is a great yoga posture to practice using muscles that need to be used, but keeping all else relaxed. Record the following sequence onto your iPod, and then get yoga-ing. If you can't read the word "buttocks" without giggling, you can download the sequence as a free podcast from my website: www.BrianLeaf.com.

Stand up with your feet shoulder-width apart and parallel to each other (see Skill 5 if you don't remember the word "parallel"). Press the crown of your head up toward the ceiling—chin parallel to the ground. Beginning with your arms at your sides, inhale as you slowly raise your arms up overhead (as though flapping wings) and exhale as you slowly lower them. Repeat this four more times, slowly moving your arms up and down, coordinating your breath with the movement. . . . Then next time your arms are over-head, hold them there. Press your feet into the ground. Press your crown up toward the ceiling—chin parallel to the floor. Press your fingertips up toward the ceiling, simultane-ously relaxing your shoulders. And breathe deep, slow breaths. Hold this posture for 10 breaths. As you hold the posture, notice where you are straining. See if you can relax. Your muscles are working to hold your arms up, but your face, feet, buttocks, and legs can be relaxed. Soften your facial muscles. Relax your belly, relax your feet, and relax your neck. Practice being focused and alert, giving your all to the task, and yet being relaxed and soft. Being relaxed frees up more energy for the task at hand and improves your performance, while simultaneously reducing strain and stress, a pretty good trad-eoff. It conserves energy and increases endurance.

Now, slowly lower your arms as you exhale. Then close your eyes and tune in to how you feel. Notice your muscles. Where do you feel strain? Now that they are no longer working to keep your arms up, see if you can allow your shoulders, back, and neck to relax and soften. Breathe a few deep breaths. Allowing your muscles to relax even more with each breath. . . . Then open your eyes and return to SAT prep relaxed, renewed, and ready to absorb new knowledge.

Set the intention to notice your muscles as you go about your day. Notice when muscles that need not be activated are tense, such as clenching a fist during SAT prep, and allow them to relax, unclench, and soften. This will reduce your stress, increase your endur-ance, and boost your performance. It will even allow you to retain more as you learn! You are a SAT ninja.

Guided Relaxation

Record the following sequence onto your iPod. Then lie back and let go. If you can't read it without giggling, you can download the sequence as a free podcast from my website: www.BrianLeaf.com.

Lie down on your back and close your eyes.

Take slow, deep breaths. Bring your awareness to your feet. Allow your feet to relax, like a fist unclenching.

Bring your awareness to your calves and shins. Let the muscles relax and soften and unclench.

Bring your awareness to your thighs and hips. Allow the thighs and hips to relax and unclench.

Bring your awareness to your whole legs. Allow the legs to relax even more, to soften even more. Allow all the muscles to drop, allow yourself to be fully supported by the floor.

Now, bring your awareness to your pelvis. Allow your pelvis to relax, to unclench and to drop and be supported by the floor.

Bring your awareness to your lower back. Allow your lower back to relax and drop.

Bring your awareness to your belly. Allow your belly to relax, to unclench, to let go.

Bring your awareness to your upper back and chest. Allow your upper back and chest to relax, to unclench. . . .

Bring your awareness to your neck, the front, sides, and back. Allow your neck to relax, to unclench, and to soften. . . .

Bring your awareness to your face: eyes, nose, mouth, and cheeks. Allow your face to soften, to relax, to unclench. . . .

Bring your awareness to your scalp. Allow your scalp to relax.

Now bring your attention to your whole body: feet, legs, pelvis, belly, back, chest, neck, head. Allow all your muscles to relax even more, to unclench even more. Allow all your muscles to soften and drop even more, allowing your whole body to be supported by the floor. . . .

Now relax a few minutes.

(Let 2 minutes pass on the recording. You can sample relaxing music here, probably not DMX.)

Now, gently begin to deepen the breath.

Take slow, deep breaths.

Wiggle the fingers and toes.

Slowly roll over to your right side and open your eyes.

Slowly sit up and make the intention to bring this feeling of relaxation and calm into all your activities: school, math homework, socializing, eating, sleeping, and of course SAT prep.

"Is" Means Equals . . . Translation

I love translation questions. It's like you are translating Spanish to English. On the SAT we are translating English to math and here is our dictionary:

"what number"	means	x
"37 percent"	means	0.37
"of" and "product"	mean	multiply
"less"	means	minus
"sum" or "more than"	means	plus
"quotient"	means	divide
"is"	means	equals
"is to" or "per"	means	divide (ratio) and often a proportion
"twice a number"	means	$2x$

Simply translate, word for word.

Here's the question from the Pretest.

26. If 20 percent of 10 percent of a number is 24 less than half the number, what is the number?

Solution: First translate. Then use algebra to solve.

$(0.20)(0.10)(n) = 0.5n - 24$	translate
$0.02n = 0.5n - 24$	multiply $(0.20)(0.10)$
$24 = 0.48n$	add 24 to both sides, and subtract $0.02n$ from both sides
$50 = n$	divide both sides by 0.48

Correct answer: 50

SAT Math Mantra #26
Translate word problems from English to math.

Let's try it, come along, children. . . .

"Is" Means Equals . . . Translation Drills

Easy

> The product of b and 2 is equal to the sum of b and $\dfrac{2}{3}$.

1 Which of the following is an expression for the relationship described above?

Ⓐ $b - 2 = b + \dfrac{2}{3}$

Ⓑ $b - 2 = \dfrac{2}{3}b$

Ⓒ $2b = b + \dfrac{2}{3}$

Ⓓ $2b = b - \dfrac{2}{3}$

Medium

2 How many inches are there in f feet and c inches?

Ⓐ $12(f + c)$

Ⓑ $12f + c$

Ⓒ $f + \dfrac{c}{12}$

Ⓓ $\dfrac{f + c}{12}$

3 When the number p is added to 6, the result is the same as when p is multiplied by 5. What is the value of $8p$?

Ⓐ $\dfrac{5}{6}$

Ⓑ 3

Ⓒ 8

Ⓓ 12

4 Nona bought a sweater in Thornes Market for $50. This included an 8% sales tax. To the nearest cent, what was the price of the sweater before sales tax?

Hard

5 If $2x + 3y$ is equal to 120 percent of $5y$, what is the value of $\dfrac{y}{x}$?

6 If the square of $(m + 11)$ equals the product of $(m + 1)^2$ and 9, what is the value of m ?

Ⓐ 4

Ⓑ 3

Ⓒ 2

Ⓓ 1

Just Do It! ... Springboard

When approaching a question, students often say, "I have no idea where to start!" This book, and this strategy especially, tells you where to start.

> **SAT Math Mantra #27**
> **When something can be factored, FOILed, reduced, or simplified, ... do it.**

Examples:

- When you see $x^2 - y^2$, **factor** it to $(x - y)(x + y)$.
- Note: $x^2 - y^2 = (x - y)(x + y)$ is the SAT's favorite kind of factoring. Memorize it!
- When you see $(x - 3)(x + 2)$, **FOIL** it to get $x^2 - x - 6$.
- When you see $\dfrac{12}{16}$, **reduce** it to $\dfrac{3}{4}$.
- When you see $\sqrt{50}$, **simplify** it to $5\sqrt{2}$ or just 7.07.

This is what the SAT wants you to do; these steps will usually bring you to the correct answer. I have seen this strategy dramatically help students, especially kids who get stuck and don't know what to do next—this strategy tells you what to do next.

> Let's look at the question from the Pretest.
>
> **27.** If $x^2 - y^2 = 36$ and $x - y = 12$, what is the value of $x + y$?

Solution: If you see $x^2 - y^2$, factor it.

$x^2 - y^2 = 36$

$(x - y)(x + y) = 36$ factor $x^2 - y^2$ to $(x - y)(x + y)$

$12(x + y) = 36$ substitute in 12 for $(x - y)$, since $(x - y) = 12$

$x + y = 3$ divide both sides by 12

Correct answer: 3

Just Do It! . . . Springboard Drills

Medium

1 If $\dfrac{3}{18} = \dfrac{a}{k}$ and a and k are integers, then k could equal which of the following?

  Ⓐ 1
  Ⓑ 3
  Ⓒ 4
  Ⓓ 6

2 If $m = p(p + 2)$, then $m - 3 =$

  Ⓐ $p^2 - 2p$
  Ⓑ $p^2 + 2$
  Ⓒ $p^2 - 2p - 3$
  Ⓓ $p^2 + 2p - 3$

3 If $x^2 - y^2 = 108$ and $x + y = 9$, what is the value of $x - y$?

Hard

4 If m and n are constants and $x^2 + mx + 5$ equals $(x + n)(x + 1)$, what is the value of m ?

  Ⓐ 5
  Ⓑ 6
  Ⓒ 7
  Ⓓ 8

5 If $12\sqrt{12} = p\sqrt{q}$ and p and q are positive integers, where $p > q$, what is the value of $\dfrac{p}{q}$?

  Ⓐ 1
  Ⓑ 4
  Ⓒ 8
  Ⓓ 16

6 If $xy = 11$, $x^2 = 5$, and $y^2 = 7$, then $(x - 3y)^2 =$

  Ⓐ 0
  Ⓑ 2
  Ⓒ 35
  Ⓓ 121

Beyond Your Dear Aunt Sally: The Laws of Exponents I

The SAT loves to test the laws of exponents. I know that you think that the SAT is incapable of love, that they are a sadistic organization. But I used to teach yoga to the employees who make the SAT, and I can tell you that they are very **nearly** normal people.

Anyway, the SAT loves exponents; they are on every test. Memorize these rules. Practice working with them in the drills, and check your answers. Then teach them to a friend.

$n^6 \times n^2 = n^8$ When multiplying like bases, add exponents.

$\dfrac{n^6}{n^2} = n^4$ When dividing like bases, subtract exponents.

$(n^6)^2 = n^{12}$ Power to a power, multiply exponents.

$n^0 = 1$ Any base to the 0 power equals 1.

SAT Math Mantra #28
Memorize the laws of exponents.

Let's look at the question from the Pretest.

28. If m, n, and p are positive integers and $3^m \cdot 3^n \cdot 3^p = 81$, then the greatest possible value for p is

(A) 1   (B) 2   (C) 3   (D) 4

Solution: Great SAT strategy: If you want one thing to be as big as possible, make the other things as small as possible. To maximize p, make m and n as small as possible. Since they must be positive, $m = n = 1$. So $3^1 \cdot 3^1 \cdot 3^p = 81$. Then "Use the Answers" and your calculator to see which answer choice works.

Correct answer: B

Easy

1 What is the product of x^2 and $2x^3$?

Ⓐ $2x^5$

Ⓑ $2x^6$

Ⓒ $3x^5$

Ⓓ $4x^6$

2 What is the product of $3m^4$ and $2b^4$?

Ⓐ $5mb^8$

Ⓑ $6mb^8$

Ⓒ $6(mb)^4$

Ⓓ $5(mb)^8$

Medium

3 If a and b are positive integers and $2^a \cdot 2^b = 64$, then the greatest possible value for b is

Ⓐ 5

Ⓑ 4

Ⓒ 3

Ⓓ 2

4 If m, n, and p are different positive integers and $2^m \cdot 2^n \cdot 2^p = 128$, then the greatest possible value for p is

Ⓐ 1

Ⓑ 2

Ⓒ 3

Ⓓ 4

5 If $p^m \cdot p^6 = p^{12}$ and $(p^3)n = p^{21}$, what is the value of $n - m$?

Ⓐ 1

Ⓑ 2

Ⓒ 5

Ⓓ 12

Hard

6 If $a^4 = b^8$, what is the value of b in terms of a ?

Ⓐ $a^{\frac{1}{2}}$

Ⓑ $2a$

Ⓒ a^2

Ⓓ $(2a)^2$

Far Beyond Your Dear Aunt Sally: The Laws of Exponents II

$n^{-2} = \dfrac{1}{n^2}$ A negative exponent means "take the reciprocal."

$2n^2 + n^2 = 3n^2$ When adding with like bases and like exponents, add coefficients. Remember that n^2 means $1\,n^2$.

$2n + n^2$ These do not combine. Terms combine only if they have like bases and like exponents.

$n^{\frac{3}{4}} = \sqrt[3]{n^4}$ For a fractional exponent, the top number is the power and the bottom number is the root.

Now, let's take a look at the question from the Pretest.

29. If $8m^2p^3 = m^5p$, what is m in terms of p ?

    (A) $p^{\frac{2}{3}}$ (B) $2p^{\frac{2}{3}}$ (C) $8p^{\frac{2}{3}}$ (D) $2p^2$

Solution: Great review of Skill 2, "What is m in terms of p" means solve for m, use algebra to get m alone.

$8m^2p^3 = m^5p$ divide both sides by p

$8m^2p^2 = m^5$ divide both sides by m^2

$8p^2 = m^3$ put both sides to the one-third exponent, since $\left(m^3\right)^{\frac{1}{3}} = m$

$\left(8p^2\right)^{\frac{1}{3}} = m$ distribute the exponent

$2p^{\frac{2}{3}} = m$

Correct answer: B

SAT Math Mantra #29
Memorize these laws of exponents, too.

    1. $n^{-2} = n^{\frac{1}{2}}$ **2.** $2n^2 + n^2 = 3n^2$ **3.** $n^{\frac{3}{4}} = \sqrt[3]{n^4}$

Medium

1 What is the sum of $2x^2$ and $2x^3$?

(A) $4x^5$

(B) $2x^6$

(C) $2x^2 + 2x^3$

(D) $2x^4 + 2x^4$

2 What is the sum of $4x^2$ and $5x^2$?

(A) $9x^4$

(B) $9x^2$

(C) $4x^2 + 5x^2$

(D) $20x^4$

3 The product of $3m^{-2}$ and $2m^{-5}$ is

(A) $\dfrac{6}{m^7}$

(B) $\dfrac{1}{6m^7}$

(C) $5m^7$

(D) $6m^7$

Hard

4 If n and p are positive integers and $3^{n/p} = \sqrt{27}$, then the product of n and p is

(A) -1

(B) 0

(C) 3

(D) 6

5 If $pm \cdot p^{-4} = p^5$ and $(p^{-2})^n = p^{20}$, what is the value of $n - m$?

(A) -1

(B) -2

(C) -5

(D) -19

6 If m, n, and p are negative integers and $3^m \cdot 3^n \cdot 3^p = (243)^{-1}$, then nmp could equal

(A) -1 or -2

(B) -2 or -3

(C) -3 or -4

(D) -4 or -5

In school, we usually use $y = mx + b$ for the equation of a line. For some reason, the SAT often uses $y = ax + b$ and this confuses students. Just know that it's the same. This is the kind of thing that can throw someone. But remember, by the time you are done with this workbook, you will know everything you need for the test; there are no surprises. Be confident. Don't be intimidated; know what you know. I'm not telling you to be arrogant, just self-assured. If you feel yourself getting thrown, relax your body, breathe deeply, chill, use your math mantras, and figure it out—you are a math ninja!

For the equation $y = mx + b$ or $y = ax + b$, m or a is the slope, sometimes called the rate of change, and b is the y intercept (the place where the line crosses the y-axis). Often this knowledge is enough to get a question correct.

Note: If you are given a point (x, y) and the equation of a line, usually you need to plug the point into the equation and solve for a variable.

SAT Math Mantra #30
For the equation $y = mx + b$ or $y = ax + b$, m or a is the slope
and b is the y intercept.

Let's take a look at the question from the Pretest.

30. If McLovin's lawn-mowing service charges $25 to come to a house and $0.50 for each bag of leaves that they remove, which of the following equations express McLovin's fees for a visit if they remove x bags of leaves?

(A) $y = 25$

(B) $y = 25x + 0.5$

(C) $y = 0.5x$

(D) $y = 0.5x + 25$

Solution: This is a great question to review because I see it in a lot of SATs lately. The fee for each bag, $0.50, is the amount that depends on the number of bags, so that goes next to the x, whereas $25 is a fixed fee, unrelated to how many bags McLovin's hauls. So $y = 0.50x + 25$.

Correct answer: D

Your Algebra Teacher Never Said "$y = ax + b$" Drills

Note: The following questions are out of Easy, Medium, Hard order because of the length of number 5 and available room on the page.

Easy

1 If a movie offends 50 people in a theater just by the title of the movie, and 25 more people with each joke, which of the following equations expresses the number of people offended after x number of jokes?

Ⓐ $y = 50$

Ⓑ $y = 50x + 25$

Ⓒ $y = 25x + 50$

Ⓓ $y = 25x$

2 If $(2, g)$ is a solution to the equation $y = -2x + 3$, then what does g equal?

Hard

3 If the equation of line j is $y = mx - 2$ and line k is perpendicular to line j at the point $(2, 1)$, what is the equation of line k?

Ⓐ $y = 2x + 3$

Ⓑ $y = \dfrac{4}{3}x - \dfrac{1}{3}$

Ⓒ $y = \dfrac{2}{3}x$

Ⓓ $y = -\dfrac{2}{3}x + \dfrac{7}{3}$

Medium

4 A researcher determined that at a given time after low tide, ocean depth at a certain location could be estimated by the equation $D = 600 + 0.05T$, in which D represents ocean depth and T represents minutes after low tide. What is the best interpretation of the number 600 in this equation?

Ⓐ The number of minutes before low tide

Ⓑ The depth at low tide

Ⓒ The depth at high tide

Ⓓ The number of hours since low tide

5 For the equation $y = ax + b$, Alex knew that b should be 4 and that the slope was positive. Which of the following could be the graph of this line?

Ⓐ
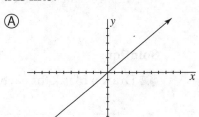

Ⓑ
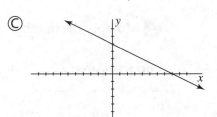

Ⓒ
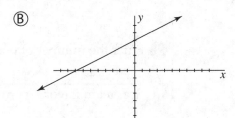

Ⓓ
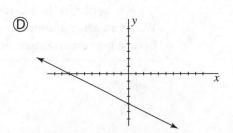

Arrangements

Arrangement questions ask you how many arrangements of something are possible, like how many different ways four letters can be arranged. These questions seem impossible to many students, but they are easy if you know the steps:

Step 1. Draw a blank for each position.
Step 2. Write in the number of possibilities to fill each position. If there are any restricted positions, fill those positions first.
Step 3. Multiply.
Step 4. If there are teams of two, divide by 2. If there are teams of three, divide by 6.

Let's take this strategy for a spin on the question from the Pretest.

31. Fletch F. Fletch buys an ice cream sundae that contains one scoop of ice cream, one sauce, and either a cherry or pineapple wedge on top. He can choose chocolate, vanilla, strawberry, or banana ice cream; he can choose chocolate, caramel, or berry sauce; and he can choose either the cherry or the pineapple wedge for the top. How many different arrangements of these ingredients for Fletch's ice cream sundae are possible?

Solution:

1 Draw a blank for each position.

$$\underset{\text{ice cream flavor}}{\underline{\hspace{3cm}}} \times \underset{\text{syrup flavor}}{\underline{\hspace{3cm}}} \times \underset{\text{cherry or pineapple}}{\underline{\hspace{3cm}}}$$

2 Enter the number of possibilities that can fill each position.

$$\underset{\text{ice cream flavor}}{\underline{\hspace{1cm}4\hspace{1cm}}} \times \underset{\text{syrup flavor}}{\underline{\hspace{1cm}3\hspace{1cm}}} \times \underset{\text{cherry or pineapple}}{\underline{\hspace{1cm}2\hspace{1cm}}}$$

3 Multiply the numbers to get the number of arrangements! $4 \times 3 \times 2 = 24$.

Correct answer: 24

SAT Math Mantra #31
When you see an arrangement question, draw a blank for each position,
write in the number of possibilities to fill each position, and multiply.
When an arrangement question mentions a "restriction," fill in the restricted positions
first. When an arrangement question mentions a "team of two," divide your result by 2.

Arrangements Drills

Easy

1 For a fundraiser, the meditation club is selling tee-shirts with a choice of two slogans, "See clearly" or "Non-attachment." Each shirt is available in small, medium, or large. How many different types of shirts are available?

2 Five actors are being cast to fill five roles. If each actor plays only one role, how many different arrangements of actors in the five roles are possible?

Ⓐ 5
Ⓑ 10
Ⓒ 60
Ⓓ 120

Medium

3 Of the six members of the girls' tennis club, two will compete as the doubles team. How many different such teams of two girls are possible?

4 The four digits 1, 2, 3, and 4 are used to form a number in which no digit is used more than once. How many such numbers are possible?

Ⓐ 4
Ⓑ 16
Ⓒ 24
Ⓓ 36

5 How many different three-digit positive integers have only prime numbers as digits?

Hard

6 How many four-digit positive integers are even?

Ⓐ 450
Ⓑ 625
Ⓒ 4,500
Ⓓ 5,000

$$\varphi \ \gamma \ \phi \ \lambda \ \varpi$$

7 The five symbols above are written so that γ is never in the middle; it is always on one of the ends. How many such arrangements are possible?

8 There are 6 kids waiting to be chosen to fill the five positions in a stickball game. If, of the 6 kids, only 3 are skilled enough to pitch or catch, how many arrangements of the 6 kids in the five positions are possible?

Ⓐ 72
Ⓑ 120
Ⓒ 144
Ⓓ 720

"Problems" is a bad name for these; they are definitely no-problems. I know some kids who see a long word problem and shut down; "I hate these; I have no chance," they say. So untrue! Long word problems on the SAT can be intimidating, but once you get past that, the actual math is easy. Usually there's some simple translation (See Skill 26) buried under lots of other words. And anyway, imagine you're a soccer goalie. What if you analyzed every ball that came at you, assessing whether you have a chance or not. You'd wind up watching a lot of balls go past. Go for every ball, every question. I'm not telling you to spend 7 minutes on one question, just to ask yourself, which Skill can I use for this question, what's the easy way to get it? You'll get more of them right, even ones you thought you had no chance on. Intimidation is the only thing standing in your way. So go for it.

Here's the question from the Pretest:

$A = P(1 + r)^{tn}$

32. The formula above is used to calculate compound interest. A represents the amount of money accumulated after n years, including interest; P is the initial principal amount (i.e., the initial amount deposited); r stands for the annual rate of interest as a decimal; and t represents the number of years and n the number of times the interest is compounded per year. If Sal deposits $100 in an account earning 6% annual interest and keeps the money in his account for five years, how much money will he have at the end of the five years? Round your answer to the nearest dollar.

    (A) 30
    (B) 130
    (C) 133
    (D) 134

Solution: This is a very common type question on the test. It appears to be an offensively long word problem. "Wait, am I in the reading comprehension section?" you might ask. But most of the word problem just describes the equation. Once you realize that, you just plug the given numbers into the equation and solve for the unknown. Then it's too easy!

$A = P(1 + r)^{tn}$

$A = 100(1 + 0.06)^{(5)(1)}$

$A = 133.82$

Rounding to the nearest dollar, we get $134.

Correct answer: D

SAT Math Mantra #32
Word problems are no-problem; translate English to math, plug numbers into the equation, and change fractions into decimals.

Let's practice.

Long Word No-Problems Drills

Easy

1 Peter and Stacey own a farm. On market day, corn sells for $0.35 per pound and tomatoes sell for $0.74 per pound. This year they grew 5,000 pounds of corn and 10,000 pounds of tomatoes. If they sell 90% of their crops, what is their total revenue, rounded to the nearest penny?

- (A) $8,235
- (B) $9,150
- (C) $10,065
- (D) $11,964

2 Joe recently contracted with a new pay-per-view company and pays $65 per year for pay-per-view access. The service charges $5 for every 3 movies he watches, which is a significant discount compared to other pay-per-view services. Last year, Joe watched 492 pay-per-view movies. What was the total cost that he paid to pay-per-view last year?

- (A) $65
- (B) $820
- (C) $885
- (D) $1,473

3 Laurie ran $3\frac{4}{5}$ miles on Tuesday and $4\frac{2}{3}$ miles on Wednesday. The total distance, in miles, that Laurie ran during those two days is within which of the following ranges?

- (A) At least $7\frac{1}{8}$ and less than $7\frac{4}{5}$
- (B) At least $7\frac{2}{5}$ and less than $7\frac{4}{5}$
- (C) At least $8\frac{1}{8}$ and less than $8\frac{1}{4}$
- (D) At least $8\frac{2}{5}$ and less than $8\frac{2}{3}$

4 Alfred bought 3 cases of blueberries. Each case contained 12 2-pint containers. Alfred could have bought the same amount of berries by buying how many 3-pint containers of berries?

- (A) 12
- (B) 18
- (C) 24
- (D) 36

$$A = P(1 + r)^{tn}$$

5 The formula above is used to calculate compound interest. A represents the amount of money accumulated after n years, including interest; P is the initial principal amount (i.e., the initial amount deposited); r stands for the annual rate of interest as a decimal; and t represents the number of years and n the number of times the interest is compounded per year. If Serina deposits $500 in an account earning 5% interest compounded semiannually and keeps the money in her account for three years, how much money will she have at the end of the five years? Round your answer to the nearest dollar.

- (A) $515.00
- (B) $530.00
- (C) $670.05
- (D) $710.10

Tell Me What You Want, What You Really, Really Want . . . Probability

They don't take the SAT over there in England, but Scary, Baby, Ginger, Posh, and Sporty summed up probability in 1996. Like functions, probability could be the topic of a college course, but the SAT asks only one thing! To find out about that one thing, please get out your credit card and visit my website.

I'm kidding. The one thing is $\quad \text{Probability} = \dfrac{\text{want}}{\text{total}}$

In English that's "Probability equals what you want, divided by the total number of things you are choosing from." Thanks again to Scary, Baby, and the gang.

Let's look at that on the Pretest.

33. Of the 24 chocolates in a box, 10 are solid milk chocolates, 10 are solid dark chocolates, and 4 are cream-filled. If Noah randomly chooses a chocolate from the box, what is the probability that it will NOT be solid dark chocolate?

(A) $\dfrac{1}{12}$ (B) $\dfrac{1}{6}$ (C) $\dfrac{5}{12}$ (D) $\dfrac{7}{12}$

Solution: Anytime you see "probability," use the equation $\text{Probability} = \dfrac{\text{want}}{\text{total}}$. We want anything but solid dark chocolate, so there are 14 we'd be happy with and that number goes on top. The total number of chocolates to choose from is 24, so that number goes on bottom. So the probability of not selecting a solid dark chocolate is $\dfrac{14}{24} = \dfrac{7}{12}$.

Correct answer: D

Probability in school could be much harder than that, but it's NEVER harder on the SAT. $\text{Probability} = \dfrac{\text{want}}{\text{total}}$ is all they ask!

SAT Math Mantra #33
When you see "probability," use the equation $\text{Probability} = \dfrac{\text{want}}{\text{total}}$.

The graph of the equation $y = ax^2 + bx + c$ forms a U shape called a parabola. The equation is called "quadratic," which is just fancy vocab for having an x^2 term. In this equation, the a tells whether the U-shaped graph opens up or down, and the c is the y-intercept, the place where the graph crosses the y-axis.

The SAT might give a quadratic equation in:

standard form, $y = ax^2 + bx + c$

vertex form, $y = a(x - h)^2 + k$, in which the vertex is (h, k)

or intercept form, $y = a(x - m)(x - n)$, in which the x-intercepts are $(m, 0)$ and $(n, 0)$.

In all three equations, the a tells whether the U-shaped graph opens up or down. The vertex is the highest or lowest point of the graph and is therefore also called the maximum or minimum point.

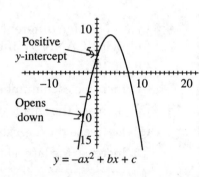

$y = -ax^2 + bx + c$

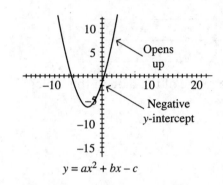

$y = ax^2 + bx - c$

Let's look at the question from the Pretest.

35. If the graph of $y = ax^2 + bx + c$ is shown on the right, then the value of ac could be

   I. Positive
   II. Negative
   III. 0

(A) I only   (B) II only   (C) I or II   (D) I or III

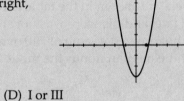

Solution: Great question! From the diagram, we can tell that the U opens up, so the value of a must be positive, and the y intercept is negative, so c is negative. Thus, $(a)(c)$ must be negative, since a positive number times a negative number equals a negative number: $(+)(-) = (-)$.

Correct answer: B

Easy

1 If 4 out of 12 marbles in a bag are blue, what is the probability that a marble selected at random from the bag will be blue?

Ⓐ $\frac{5}{6}$

Ⓑ $\frac{1}{3}$

Ⓒ $\frac{2}{3}$

Ⓓ $\frac{3}{4}$

Medium

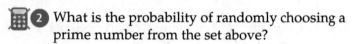
$\{1, 4, 5, 6, 7, 8\}$

2 What is the probability of randomly choosing a prime number from the set above?

3 A vegetable is to be chosen at random from a basket of vegetables. The probability that the vegetable chosen is a carrot is $\frac{1}{4}$. Which of the following could be the number of vegetables in the basket?

Ⓐ 5

Ⓑ 6

Ⓒ 7

Ⓓ 8

4 A certain movie has c scenes containing obscenities and n scenes free of obscenities. If a scene is picked at random from the movie and the probability of obscenities is $\frac{7}{12}$, what is the value of $\frac{n}{c}$?

Ⓐ $\frac{7}{5}$

Ⓑ $\frac{12}{7}$

Ⓒ $\frac{5}{7}$

Ⓓ $\frac{7}{12}$

Hard

5 In game 1 of the finals, Northampton will play Amherst. In game 2 Amherst will play Hadley. In game 3 Hadley will play Northampton. If, in each game, either team has an equal chance of winning, what is the probability that Northampton will win both its games?

6 Jacob gathers data on the wins and losses of his favorite high school tennis players. The data are summarized in the table below.

	Toula	Nikhil	Total
Wins in Northampton	10	11	21
Wins in Hadley	15	11	26
Total	25	22	47

If Jacob plans to rewatch on video one of the games that was won in Northampton, what is the probability that Toula won that game?

Ⓐ 10%

Ⓑ 47.6%

Ⓒ 53.2%

Ⓓ 100%

34

He's Making a List . . .
Median, Mode, and Range

He's Making a List . . . Median and Mode Drills

Median, mode, and range questions test one thing. They test whether you know the words "median," "mode," and "range." Know the terms, and you will get these questions right every time.

> **Median** is the middle number in a list of numbers.
> **Mode** is the number that occurs the most often.
> **Range** is the largest minus the smallest number.

Consider this list: 5, 7, 9, 9, 11, 12, 12, 15, 15, 15, 15.
The median is 12 (it's in the middle of the list).
The mode is 15 (it occurs most often, 4 times).
The range is 10 (15 − 5 = 10).
That's it. It's that easy.

When you see a median or mode question:

- If the list of numbers is not in order, rewrite the numbers in order, from lowest to highest.
- If the numbers are given in a table, rewrite them as a list.
- Remember that increasing the value of any number above the median does not change the median.
- Also remember that decreasing the value of any number below the median does not

> Let's take a look at the question from the Pretest.
>
> **34.** The median of a set of nine consecutive integers is 42. What is the greatest of these nine numbers?

change the median.

Solution: Simply draw blanks for the nine numbers and place 42 in the middle blank. Then fill in the consecutive numbers above and below 42. "Consecutive" means numbers in a row, for example, 42, 43, 44, 45, 46. So the greatest number is 46.

Correct answer: 46

SAT Math Mantra #34
When you see "median," "mode," or "range," rewrite the data as a list in order , from lowest to highest.

Medium

1 The median of a set of seven consecutive numbers is 31. What is the smallest of these seven numbers?

Questions 2 and 3 use the table below.

Score	Number of Bowlers
150	2
145	3
140	1
135	2
130	4
125	2

2 What is the range of the data in the table?

3 The scores on Wednesday's Bowling League for 14 bowlers are shown in the table above. Don finished late, and his score was not shown in the table. If he received a score of 140, what is the value of the median minus the mode?

Ⓐ 5
Ⓑ 10
Ⓒ 15
Ⓓ 20

Hard

4 If $2m - 2$, $m + 3$, and $3m - 4$ are all integers and $2m - 2$ is the mode of these integers, which of the following could be a value for m ?

Ⓐ 2
Ⓑ 4
Ⓒ 6
Ⓓ 8

5 In a set of nine different numbers, which of the following CANNOT affect the value of the median?

Ⓐ Increase each number by 4.
Ⓑ Increase the smallest number only.
Ⓒ Decrease the largest number only.
Ⓓ Increase the largest number only.

Week	Attendance
1	531
2	452
3	x
4	357
5	389

6 The table above shows attendance at school football games for the past five weeks. If no two weeks had the same attendance and the median attendance for the five weeks was 452, what is the least possible value of x ?

Also, remember from Skill 30, when you are given a point (x, y) and an equation, plug the point into the equation.

$y = ax^2 + bx + c$ Drills

Medium

1 In the xy coordinate system, the graph of $y = 2x^2 + 3x + 4$ intersects $y = -x^2 + 3x + 4$ at $(0, k)$. What is the value of k?

Ⓐ 5

Ⓑ 4

Ⓒ 3

Ⓓ 2

2 What are the coordinates for the maximum point in the graph of $y - 2 = -(x + 3)^2$?

Ⓐ $-(3, 2)$

Ⓑ $-(-3, 2)$

Ⓒ $-(3, -2)$

Ⓓ $-(-3, -2)$

3 Which of the following functions in the xy-plane has x-intercepts at 3 and -2?

Ⓐ $f(x) - (x + 3)(x - 2)$

Ⓑ $f(x) - (x - 3)(x + 2)$

Ⓒ $f(x) - (x + 3)^2 - 2$

Ⓓ $f(x) - (x + 2)^2 + 3$

4 When $y = 0$, what is the positive value of x in the equation below?

$$y - 5x^2 - 10x + 15$$

5 When $y = 0$, what is the positive value of x in the equation below?

$$y - 5x^2 - 10x + 12$$

6 The equation $h = -4.9t^2 + 20t$ expresses the height, h, in feet, of a ball t seconds after it is thrown vertically upward from the ground with an initial velocity of 20 feet per second. After how many seconds (rounded to the nearest whole number) will the ball hit the ground?

Hard

7 In the xy coordinate system, the graph of $y = 2x^2 + 3x + 4$ intersects $y = -x^2 + 3x + 4$ at $(m, 4)$. How many values for m satisfy the above equation?

Ⓐ 0

Ⓑ 1

Ⓒ 2

Ⓓ 3

8 In the xy coordinate system, the graph of functions $f(x) = 2x^2 + 4$ intersects $g(x) = -x^2 - k$ at $(m, 22)$. If m and k are integers, what is the value of k?

Ⓐ -31

Ⓑ -3

Ⓒ 0

Ⓓ 31

9 Which of the following could be the graph of $y = kx^2 + 3x + r$, if k and r are negative constants?

Ⓐ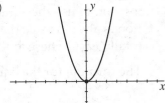

Ⓑ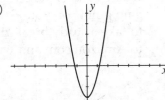

Ⓒ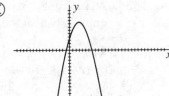

Ⓓ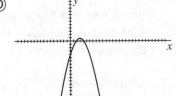

Circles

I love this Skill. Yes, I do. And I'll tell you why. Almost every SAT has one question asking you to use the equation of a circle. Nobody has this thing memorized, so the question is always ranked as a "medium," or even a "hard." But if you know the formula, it's totally easy! These are the best.

The formula for the equation of a circle is

$$(x - h)^2 + (y - k)^2 = r^2$$

where (h, k) is the center of the circle and r is the radius. Memorize this, and you will gain points on your SAT score, guaranteed. Don't you love this book! In fact, I want you to take a study break right now to call two friends and recommend this book. Or, log on to Amazon.com and write a rave review expressing your gratitude and appreciation!

Let's look at the Pretest question.

36. A circle in the standard (x, y) coordinate plane has center (4, 2) and radius 5 coordinate units. Which of the following is an equation of the circle?

(A) $(x - 4)^2 - (y - 2)^2 = 5$
(B) $(x + 4)^2 + (y + 2)^2 = 5$
(C) $(x - 4)^2 + (y - 2)^2 = 25$
(D) $(x - 4)^2 + (y + 2)^2 = 25$

Solution: The center is (4, 2), so $h = 4$ and $k = 2$. Plus, the radius is 5, so $r = 5$. Easy. Plug that into the equation for a circle, $(x - h)^2 + (y - k)^2 = r^2$, which you have memorized. So the answer is C, or $(x - 4)^2 + (y - 2)^2 = 25$. Easy points!

Correct answer: C

SAT Math Mantra #36
The equation for a circle is $(x - h)^2 + (y - k)^2 = r^2$, where (h, k) is the center and r is the radius of the circle.

Circle Drills

Medium

1 Which of the following best describes all points in a plane that are 8 inches from a given point in the plane?

    Ⓐ A circle with an 8-inch radius

    Ⓑ A circle with an 8-inch diameter

    Ⓒ A circle with a 2-inch radius

    Ⓓ A rectangle with 8-inch sides

2 What is the center of the circle given by the equation $(x - 8)^2 + (y + 2)^2 = 49$?

    Ⓐ $(8, 2)$

    Ⓑ $(-8, -2)$

    Ⓒ $(8, -2)$

    Ⓓ $(7, 7)$

3 A circle in the standard (x, y) coordinate plane has center $(5, -3)$ and radius 6 coordinate units. Which of the following is an equation of the circle?

    Ⓐ $(x - 5)^2 - (y - 3)^2 = 6$

    Ⓑ $(x + 5)^2 + (y + 3)^2 = 6$

    Ⓒ $(x - 5)^2 + (y - 3)^2 = 6$

    Ⓓ $(x - 5)^2 + (y + 3)^2 = 36$

Hard

4 Which of the following is an equation of a circle with center at $(1, 4)$ and tangent to the y-axis in the standard (x, y) coordinate plane?

    Ⓐ $x^2 + y^2 = 1$

    Ⓑ $x^2 - y^2 = 1$

    Ⓒ $(x - 1)^2 + (y - 4)^2 = 2$

    Ⓓ $(x - 1)^2 + (y - 4)^2 = 1$

5 A circle in the standard (x, y) coordinate plane is tangent to the x-axis at 3 and tangent to the y-axis at 3. Which of the following is an equation of the circle?

    Ⓐ $x^2 + y^2 = 3$

    Ⓑ $(x - 3)^2 - (y - 3)^2 = 9$

    Ⓒ $(x - 3)^2 + (y - 3)^2 = 3$

    Ⓓ $(x - 3)^2 + (y - 3)^2 = 9$

6 The graph of the equation $x^2 + 6x + y^2 - 4y = 12$ is a circle. What is the radius of the circle?

Hopscotch, Pigtails, and Remainders

Remember remainders? Back in 5th grade you had this thing down. You learned it, put it up on the fridge, and ran out into the yard for prisoner dodgeball. But now it's six years later, and you've no idea what I'm talking about.

Remainders are what's left over when you use long division.

$$
\begin{array}{r}
52\ r1 \\
7\overline{\smash{)}365} \\
-35 \\
\hline
15 \\
-14 \\
\hline
1
\end{array}
$$

For example:

The r1 means remainder 1. That's it. So why is this on the SAT? I think that years ago, when the SAT made the decision to allow calculators on the test, they started using remainder questions since they are hard to do with a calculator. But the Buddha said that if a man is shot by an arrow, do not waste time on discovering who shot him, just help him. So here's the help. Remainders are easy, and as usual, the SAT always asks the same concepts.

Let's take a look at the Pretest question.

37. All the following numbers have remainder 3 when divided by 4 EXCEPT

(A) 7   (B) 15   (C) 22   (D) 23

Solution: This is a great review of our "Use the Answers" strategy. Just try each number to see which answer choice does not give remainder 3 when divided by 4.

$$
\begin{array}{r}
1\ r3 \\
4\overline{\smash{)}7} \\
4 \\
\hline
3
\end{array}
\qquad
\begin{array}{r}
3\ r3 \\
4\overline{\smash{)}15} \\
12 \\
\hline
3
\end{array}
\qquad
\begin{array}{r}
5\ r2 \\
4\overline{\smash{)}22} \\
20 \\
\hline
2
\end{array}
\qquad
\begin{array}{r}
5\ r3 \\
4\overline{\smash{)}23} \\
20 \\
\hline
3
\end{array}
$$

Each choice works EXCEPT choice C, 22, which gives a remainder of 2, not 3.

Correct answer: C

SAT Math Mantra #37
Remainders are what's left over when you use long division.

Hopscotch, Pigtails, and Remainders Drills

Medium

1 What is the remainder when 13 is divided by 3 ?

- (A) 0
- (B) 1
- (C) 2
- (D) 3

2 All the following can be the remainders of 24 divided by an even number EXCEPT

- (A) 12
- (B) 10
- (C) 8
- (D) 6

3 All the following numbers have the same remainder when divided by 4 EXCEPT

- (A) 7
- (B) 15
- (C) 19
- (D) 22

Hard

4 Which of the following could be remainders when five consecutive positive integers are each divided by 4 ?

- (A) 1, 2, 3, 0, 1
- (B) 1, 2, 3, 4, 1
- (C) 1, 2, 0, 1, 2
- (D) 0, 1, 2, 1, 0

5 For all negative integers m and n, let $m \, \Re \, n$ be defined as the remainder when n is divided by m. If $-18 \, \Re \, n = 3$, which of the following can be the value of n ?

- (A) −18
- (B) −36
- (C) 36
- (D) 39

6 For all integers p and q, let $p \Theta q$ be defined as the remainder when p is divided by q. How many different values for b make the statement $24 \Theta b = 3$ true?

- (A) 0
- (B) 1
- (C) 2
- (D) 3

The expression |–3| means "the absolute value of –3." The || bars mean absolute value. Like many SAT topics, this is really just vocab. If you don't know the meaning of the term, then it's very hard or impossible to get the question correct; but if you know the vocab, it's EASY!

Basically, absolute value just means, "Ditch the negative sign!" |–3| = 3 and |3| = 3. So it does not mean to switch the sign necessarily; it just means drop the (–) negative signs, which makes it positive. You do this only after you've done what is between the bars. For example, $|-3 - 6| = |-9| = 9$. You don't just drop negative signs right away. First you do the math between the bars, and when you've done all the math that you can, then you drop the negative sign.

Here's the key to absolute value on the SAT: usually you have to come up with the less obvious answer to the question. For example, of course 3 is one answer to $|x - 1| = 2$, but –1 is also an answer, and that's the one you'll need on the SAT. How do you find the less obvious answer? Drop the bars and switch the sign of the answer: $x - 1 = -2$; then solve for x.

That's it. That's absolute value. If you did not know this and you do by the end of the drills, then you will gain points!

Let's practice.

38. Which of the following are solutions to $|n + 3| = 5$?

    I. 2   II. –2   III. –8

  (A) I only
  (B) III only
  (C) II and III
  (D) I and III

Solution: Great "Use the Answers" review. Try each answer choice in the absolute value equation in the question:

I. $|2 + 3| = 5$ correct   II. $|-2 + 3| = 5$ incorrect   III. $|-8 + 3| = 5$ correct

So I and III are correct and choice D is the answer.

Correct answer: D

SAT Math Mantra #38
When you see absolute value, look for the less obvious answer.

Absolute Value Drills

Easy

 1 If $|6 - m| = 12$, then $m =$

   Ⓐ 6 or 0

   Ⓑ 12 or −6

   Ⓒ 18 or −6

   Ⓓ 18 or 6

2 Which of the following are solutions to $|p - 6| = 5$?

   I. 11

   II. 5

   III. 1

   Ⓐ I only

   Ⓑ III only

   Ⓒ II and III

   Ⓓ I and III

Medium

3 For negative integers m and n, if $|m| + |n| = 8$, what is the least possible value for $m - n$?

   Ⓐ 8

   Ⓑ 0

   Ⓒ −4

   Ⓓ −6

$$|4 + x| = 8$$
$$|3 - y| = 5$$

4 If in the equations above $x < 0$ and $y < 0$, what is the value of xy?

   Ⓐ −24

   Ⓑ −12

   Ⓒ 12

   Ⓓ 24

5 If $|1 + 2a| < 1$, what is one possible value of a?

Hard

6 If $m = |n|$, then m could equal

   I. 0

   II. n

   III. $-n$

   Ⓐ I and II

   Ⓑ II and III

   Ⓒ I and III

   Ⓓ I, II, and III

7 At the Three County Fair, certain kids' rides require a minimum height of 48 inches and a maximum height of 68 inches. Which of the following inequalities describes all possible heights h, in inches, that are within this range to allow a child onto these rides?

   Ⓐ $|h + 58| > 10$

   Ⓑ $|h - 58| \leq 10$

   Ⓒ $|h - 20| > 58$

   Ⓓ $|h + 20| \leq 58$

I love to teach these. Many kids don't know much about sequences, but they are super easy to learn and easy to get right once you know the Skill. They are easy points to add to your SAT score.

The SAT uses two vocab words that you need to know:

1 Arithmetic sequence—a sequence of numbers where a certain number is added to each term to arrive at the next, like 3, 7, 11, 15, 19, . . .

The number 4 is added to each term to arrive at the next.

2 Geometric sequence—a sequence of numbers where a certain number is multiplied by each term to arrive at the next, like 3, −6, 12, −24, 48, . . .

The number −2 is multiplied by each term to get the next.

The SAT asks you to do two things with these. They ask you to either predict the next term or predict the sum of a bunch of terms. There is a complex formula to do this that you may or may not have used in school, but on the SAT we don't need it. Just figure out the number being added or multiplied and write out as many terms as you need to answer the question. We'll do this on the drills.

SAT Math Mantra #39

An arithmetic sequence is a sequence of numbers where a certain number is ADDED to each term to arrive at the next, like 3, 7, 11, 15, 19.

A geometric sequence is a sequence of numbers where a certain number is MULTIPLIED by each term to arrive at the next, like 3, −6, 12, −24, 48.

Here's the question from the Pretest.

39. Which of the following is NOT true about the arithmetic sequence 20, 13, 6, −1, . . . ?

(A) The fifth term is −8.
(B) The sum of the first five terms is 30.
(C) The common ratio of consecutive terms is −7.
(D) The seventh term is −22.

Solution: When you see an arithmetic sequence, figure out the number being added to each term to get the next. Usually you can tell just by looking at it, or you can subtract: 13 − 20 = −7. So −7 is being added to each term to arrive at the next. You can even test to make sure that you are correct. Yup, 13 + (−7) = 6. So now we can predict the fifth and eighth terms, and we can calculate the sum of the first five terms. Choices A, B, and D are all correct. C is not true; −7 is the difference, not the ratio. Ratio would be for a geometric sequence.

Correct answer: C

Brian's Math Magic Trick #2
Choose a number between 1 and 10.
Multiply your number by 9.
Take the result and add the digits; for example, if your result was 26, then 2 + 6 = 8.
Now take that number and subtract 5.
Then find the letter of the alphabet that corresponds to that number: 1 is A, 2 is B, 3 is C, 4 is D, 5 is E, and so on. Choose a country that begins with that letter. Spell the country; what is the second letter? And choose an animal that begins that letter. Now turn to the solutions for Skill 39.

Sequences Drills

Easy

1 What two numbers should be placed in the blanks so that the difference between consecutive numbers is the same?

$$14, \_\_, \_\_, 47$$

- (A) 11, 11
- (B) 25, 36
- (C) 27, 38
- (D) 29, 39

2 The second term of an arithmetic sequence is –5, and the third term is 12. What is the first term?

- (A) –22
- (B) –17
- (C) 0
- (D) 17

3 What is the next term after $-\frac{1}{2}$ in the geometric sequence $4, -2, 1, -\frac{1}{2}, \ldots$?

- (A) $\frac{1}{2}$
- (B) $\frac{1}{4}$
- (C) 0
- (D) $-\frac{1}{2}$

Hard

4 Tiara earned $12 on her first day selling lemonade, and she was determined to earn $3 more each day than she had made the day before. If she met this goal exactly, how much money did she earn, in total, for her first 20 days selling lemonade?

- (A) $810
- (B) $610
- (B) $405
- (D) $72

Not So Complex Numbers

Math books call this topic *complex numbers*. Right off the bat, that's an unfortunate name. Could it be more intimidating? Who thought this name up? But that name is just fronting; complex numbers are really not very complex at all.

They are numbers that have a regular part, like 5 or –13, and an imaginary part, called i. What is i? $i = \sqrt{-1}$; that's why it's called imaginary, since $\sqrt{-1}$ does not exist. (Remember from Skill 8 that $\sqrt{-1}$ is undefined and the math police are on their way.)

Like we didn't have enough numbers already. They said, "Let's imagine up some that don't even exist." Well, at least there is only one imaginary number, i.

So complex numbers have a normal part and an i part, like $2 + 2i$. These questions, like so many, are easy once you just know what i is. The key to these questions is that $i \sqrt{-1}$ and therefore $i^2 = -1$. **So, just treat i like a normal variable, and in the final step of a question, replace i^2 with –1.** That's it.

Let's look at the question from the Pretest.

40. What is $(i-2)(i-3)$?

   (A) $5 - 5i$
   (B) $5 - 4i$
   (C) $5 + i$
   (D) 5

Solution: No problem, and great FOIL review. Just FOIL $(i-2)(i-3)$ to get $i^2 - 3i - 2i + 6$ and collect like terms to get $i^2 - 5i + 6$. With normal FOILing you'd be done, but here there is one last step, the key to complex number questions. Since i^2 actually equals –1, we substitute –1 for i^2 to get $-1 - 5i + 6$ and collect like terms to get a final answer of $5 - 5i$.

Correct answer: A

SAT Math Mantra #40
The key to complex number questions is to treat i like a normal variable and then, in the final step, replace i^2 with –1.

Not So Complex Numbers Drills

Medium

1 What is the product of $-2i$ and $(3i + 2)$?

Ⓐ -6

Ⓑ -5

Ⓒ $6 - 4i$

Ⓓ $6 + 4i$

2 What is the square of the complex number $(i - 2)$?

Ⓐ -4

Ⓑ -3

Ⓒ $3 - 4i$

Ⓓ $4 - 4i$

Medium

3 $\dfrac{6i}{2 - i} =$

Ⓐ $3i$

Ⓑ $3i - 6$

Ⓒ $\dfrac{12i - 6}{5}$

Ⓓ $4i - 2$

Hard

4 In the complex numbers, $i^4 =$

Ⓐ $\sqrt{-1}$

Ⓑ -1

Ⓒ 0

Ⓓ 1

5 In the complex numbers, $\dfrac{1}{1 - i} \cdot \dfrac{1 - i}{1 + i} =$

Ⓐ $1 - i$

Ⓑ $1 + i$

Ⓒ $\dfrac{2}{1 - i}$

Ⓓ $\dfrac{1 - i}{2}$

6 In the complex numbers, $\dfrac{5i}{1 - i} \cdot \dfrac{1 - i^2}{1 + i} =$

Ⓐ $1 - i$

Ⓑ $1 + i$

Ⓒ $-1 - i$

Ⓓ $5i$

On average, after memorizing and practicing Skills 41 and 42 for avoiding careless errors, most students gain 20 to 30 points! So learn these strategies.

Most Common SAT Math Careless Errors

1. Practice being focused, yet relaxed. You don't need to be tense and a wreck to excel on the SAT or in life. You can be intense and work quickly, yet be relaxed. Be fully present with each question: focused, relaxed, awake, and mindful. See "A Yoga Posture for the SAT," page 60.

2. $(2x)^2 = 4x^2$, not $2x^2$. Square both the 2 and the x.

3. $-2(3x - 3) = -6x + 6$, not $-6x - 6$.

   Remember to distribute the -2 to both the $3x$ and the -3.

4. $\dfrac{5x + 20}{5} = x + 4$, not $x + 20$.

   Remember that the 5 is under not only the $5x$, but also the 20.

Let's look at the Pretest question.

41. If $f(x) = 3x^2$, which of the following expresses $f(2p)$?

   (A) $6p$
   (B) $6p^2$
   (C) $12p$
   (D) $12p^2$

Solution: Nice functions review! This is SAT function question type I. The $f(2p)$ just means plug $2p$ in for x. So $f(2p) = 3(2p)^2 = 3(4p^2) = 12p^2$. CARELESS ERROR BUSTER: Remember that the 2 gets squared. Also remember order of operations: multiply 3 by 4 after squaring 2.

Correct answer: D

SAT Math Mantra #41
"Careless errors are bad mmmkay," so be fully present with each question: focused, relaxed, awake, and mindful. Oh, and also remember to distribute the negative:
$-2(3x - 3) = -6x + 6$, not $-6x - 6$.

Don't Even Think About It! . . . Most Common SAT Math Careless Errors I Drills

Medium

1 If $f(x) = -2x^3$, which of the following expresses $f(-p)$?

Ⓐ $-2p$

Ⓑ $2p3$

Ⓒ $-2p3$

Ⓓ $8p3$

2 When $m = -1$, which of the following is equivalent to $m(2x^2 - 2)$?

Ⓐ $-2x^2 + 2$

Ⓑ $-2x^2 - 2$

Ⓒ $2x^2 - 2$

Ⓓ $2x^2 + 2$

3 If $y = \dfrac{3a - 15}{x}$, find y when $x = 3$.

Ⓐ $a - 15$

Ⓑ $9a - 15$

Ⓒ $9a - 5$

Ⓓ $a - 5$

Hard

4 If $m = 2p$, then which of the following is equivalent to $(m + 4)^2$?

Ⓐ $2p + 4$

Ⓑ $4p^2 + 4$

Ⓒ $4p^2 + 16p + 16$

Ⓓ $4p^2 - 16p + 16$

5 If $f(x) = x(2x^2 - 2)$, find $f(-2p)$.

Ⓐ $-16p^3 + 4p$

Ⓑ $-8p^3 + 4p$

Ⓒ $-8p^3 - 4p$

Ⓓ $16p^3 - 4p$

Questions 6 and 7 use the two equations below.

$$f(x) = x(x - 2)$$
$$g(x) = 3x$$

6 For functions f and g above, if $g(m) = 27$, find $f(-2m)$.

7 For functions f and g above, find $g(5) - f(1)$.

Don't Even Think About It! . . . Most Common SAT Math Careless Errors II

"Careless errors are bad mmmkay." So let's learn to avoid three more of the most common ones.

1 $(x + 3)^2 = (x + 3)(x + 3) = x^2 + 6x + 9$, not $x^2 + 9$

Remember the middle term when you FOIL.

2 $2(3)^2 = 18$, not 36.

Remember your old friend PEMDAS, order of operation:

Parenthesis, Exponents, Multiplication/Division, Addition/Subtraction.

3 Remember to finish the question. Sometimes you have solved for x, but the question asks for y or $3x - 2$. So before you grid each answer, take a moment to pause and say, "Wait (insert your name here), did I finish the question?" This is so simple, but hugely important. This is the most common careless error, and it's so easy to avoid!

SAT Math Mantra #42
"Careless errors are bad mmmkay," so underline all vocabulary words and remember to finish the question.

Many students lose tons of points to careless errors. Don't do that. Memorize the above rules and practice watching for them. Be focused, relaxed, and mindful, and you will not make careless errors. You will be a math ninja, and like most ninja of ancient Japan, you will ace the SAT.

Pretest question:

42. For the equation $y = -3x^3 - 2$, when $x = 1$, what is the value of $-2y$?

Solution: When $x = 1$, $y = -3(1)^2 - 2 = -5$. CARELESS ERROR BUSTER: Remember to finish the question. The question does not ask for y, but for $-2y$. So the correct answer is $-2(-5) = 10$. This is weird since your math teacher always asks for y not $-2y$, but we know to watch for it and we avoid the careless error.

Correct answer: 10

Don't Even Think About It! . . . Most Common SAT Math Careless Errors II Drills

Medium

 1 If $f(x) = 3x^2$, which of the following expresses $f(4p)$?

Ⓐ $12p^2$

Ⓑ $32p^2$

Ⓒ $48p^2$

Ⓓ $64p^2$

$$y = 2x^2 + 4$$

2 When $x = -2$ in the equation above, what is the value of $y + 2$?

3 John rode his bicycle 5 miles to school in 10 minutes, and at the same speed, he later rode his bicycle to a friend's house 4 miles away. How many minutes would it take him to ride there?

Ⓐ 10

Ⓑ 8

Ⓒ 2

Ⓓ 1

Hard

4 If $x = 3y$, then which of the following is equivalent to $(x - 2)^2$?

Ⓐ $3y - 2$

Ⓑ $3y^2 - 4$

Ⓒ $3y^2 + 6y - 4$

Ⓓ $9y^2 - 12y + 4$

$$p(x) = 2x(x - 2)$$
$$r(x) = \frac{x}{3}$$

5 For functions p and r above, if $r(-6) = n$, find $p(-2n)$.

6 Josh rode his bicycle from his house to his grandmother's house at a rate of 10 miles per hour. Later that day he rode home at a rate of 15 miles per hour. If the round trip took a total of 30 minutes, how far does Josh live from his grandmother?

Misbehaving Numbers: Weird Number Behavior

The SAT tests your understanding of how certain weird numbers behave, such as when you subtract a negative, it's like adding, –6 is smaller than –1, and one-half squared gets smaller. You can know these, because here's the thing—the SAT always tests the same weird math behaviors. Here they are:

1 Small fractions multiplied by small fractions get smaller.

Usually when you multiply numbers, the result is larger than the originals, but small fractions get smaller.

Example: $\left(\dfrac{1}{2}\right)^2 = \dfrac{1}{2} \times \dfrac{1}{2} = \dfrac{1}{4}$

2 The larger the digits of a negative number, the smaller it actually is.

Example: $-6 < -1$

3 Subtracting a negative number is like adding.

Example: $10 - (-4) = 14$

4 Squaring a negative eliminates it, but cubing does not.

Example: $(-3)^2 = 9$, but $(-3)^3 = -27$

5 Anything times zero equals zero.

Example: $(-16)(3)(0) = 0$

That's it. Know these and you will gain points, impress friends, and in general be a more attractive person.

Let's see if you're ready to take this skill out for a spin. Here's the question from the Pretest.

43. If $0.5mno = 0$ and $4nop = 12$, then which of the following must be true?

    (A) $nop = 12$ (B) $mno = -0.5$ (C) $p = 0$ (D) $m = 0$

Solution: This is a great question. The SAT loves to see if you pick up on the zero stuff. In order to multiply to get zero, one of the numbers must be zero. And anything times zero equals zero. So $mno = 0$ and $nop \ne 0$, and therefore, m must equal zero.

Correct answer: D

> **SAT Math Mantra #43**
> Remember that small fractions multiplied by small fractions get smaller and that subtracting a negative number is like adding.

Misbehaving Numbers: Weird Number Behavior Drills

Easy

1 If $q = 2kp$ and $k = 0$, what is the value of q ?

Medium

2 On the number line above, which of the following could be represented by point N ?

Ⓐ 8

Ⓑ 4

Ⓒ −3

Ⓓ −8

3 If $(x - 2)(x + 3) = 0$, then x could equal

I. −3

II. 0

III. 2

Ⓐ II only

Ⓑ I and II

Ⓒ I and III

Ⓓ II and III

4 If $m = -2$ and $n > 0$, which of the following is greatest?

Ⓐ mn

Ⓑ m^2n

Ⓒ m^4n

Ⓓ m^5n

5 If $f(x) = 2f(x)$, then $f(x) =$

Ⓐ −1

Ⓑ 0

Ⓒ 1

Ⓓ 2

6 If $r < 0$, which of the following is greatest?

Ⓐ r

Ⓑ $2 + r$

Ⓒ $2 - r$

Ⓓ $2 - r^2$

Hard

7 If $-2 < x < -1$, then which of the following orders x, x^2, and x^3 from least to greatest?

Ⓐ $x < x^2 < x^3$

Ⓑ $x^2 < x^3 < x$

Ⓒ $x^3 < x < x^2$

Ⓓ $x < x^3 < x^2$

Mathematical Transformations

Transformations begin with a "parent" equation or graph, for example, $y = x^2$. It's called the parent because the transformed graphs are birthed/derived from it. A transformation happens when we add, subtract, multiply, or divide a number into the original that causes it to move it up, down, left, or right. It might even make it skinnier or fatter.

Here are all the transformations that the SAT uses:

$y = x^2 + 1$ moves every point of the graph up 1 unit.

$y = x^2 - 1$ moves every point of the graph down 1 unit.

$y = (x + 1)^2$ moves every point of the graph left 1 unit.

$y = (x - 1)^2$ moves every point of the graph right 1 unit.

$y = 2(x)^2$ makes the graph skinnier.

$y = 0.5(x)^2$ makes the graph fatter.

$y = -(x)^2$ reflects the graph across the x-axis.

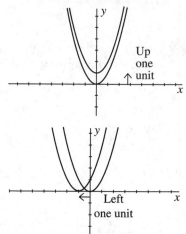

Let's practice using these:

44. The graph of $y = g(x)$ is shown below. Which of the following equations represents all the points of $g(x)$ shifted 1 unit to the left?

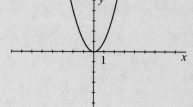

    (A) $y = g(x) + 1$
    (B) $y = g(x + 1)$
    (C) $y = g(x - 1)$
    (D) $y = g(x) - 1$

Solution: This is a straightforward transformation. The parent function $g(x)$ needs to be shifted 1 unit to the left. If you memorized the transformations shown above, this question is easy; a left transformation would be $y = g(x + 1)$. If you did not memorize the transformations, well . . . get to it, you silly slacker. Of course, you could also graph each choice on your calculator and see which one yields results that are all 1 unit to the left of the parent.

Correct answer: B

SAT Math Mantra #44
Memorize the four types of transformation notation (up/down, left/right, thinner/ thicker, reflection).

Mathematical Transformations Drills

Easy

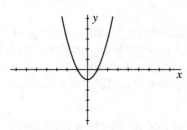

1 Which of the following could be the equation of the graph above?

- (A) $y = x - 1$
- (B) $y = x^2 - 1$
- (C) $y = (x - 1)^2$
- (D) $y = (x + 1)^2$

Medium

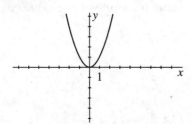

2 The graph of $g(x)$ is shown above. Which of the following equations represents all the points of $g(x)$ shifted 1 unit to the right?

- (A) $y = g(x) + 1$
- (B) $y = g(x + 1)$
- (C) $y = g(x - 1)$
- (D) $y = g(x) + 1$

Hard

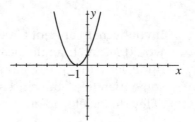

3 Which of the following could represent all the points of the above graph moved 2 units down?

- (A) $y = x - 2$
- (B) $y = x^2 - 2$
- (C) $y = (x - 1)^2 - 2$
- (D) $y = (x + 1)^2 - 2$

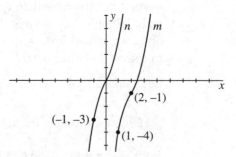

4 The figure above shows the graphs of the functions m and n. The function m is defined by $m(x) = x^3 + 2x$, and the function n is defined by $n(x) = m(x + h) - k$, where h and k are constants. What is the value of $h - k$?

- (A) 0
- (B) 1
- (C) 2
- (D) 3

SohCahToa!

If you were in ancient Greece, the word "trigonometry" would not be intimidating. It would mean "triangle measurement," and when your pal Plato came up and said, "Hey dude, let's do our trigonometry homework," you'd just hear, "Hey dude, let's measure some triangles." But since you don't live in ancient Greece, it sounds like he's saying "Hey dude, let's do our %*#$!^ homework."

But trig is just triangle measurement. It's the way that sides and angles in a triangle are related to each other. They gave these relationships names that made perfect sense in ancient Greece, but now they freak some kids out, so stay relaxed when you see the names. Here they are, and for half the SAT trig questions, they are all you need to know:

$$\sin = \frac{\text{opposite}}{\text{hypotenuse}} \qquad \cos = \frac{\text{adjacent}}{\text{hypotenuse}} \qquad \tan = \frac{\text{opposite}}{\text{adjacent}}$$

This means, for example, that the sin of an angle equals the ratio of the side opposite the angle, divided by the hypotenuse. There's a great way to remember these ratios: SohCahToa. It stands for **S**in = **O**pposite over **H**ypotenuse, **C**os = **A**djacent over **H**ypotenuse, and **T**an = **O**pposite over **A**djacent. I recommend taking a break right now and marching around the room chanting "SohCahToa." You're sure never to forget it. SohCahToa is all you need for half of the trig questions on the SAT.

Remember from Skill 24 that "hypotenuse" is just a fancy word for the longest side of a right triangle; it's always the one opposite the 90° angle. The other two sides, the shorter ones, are called *legs*. And "opposite" or "adjacent" refers to the leg opposite or adjacent to the angle being used.

Let's take a look.

Here's the question from the Pretest.

45. For right triangle △XYZ, in which the lengths of XY, YZ, and XZ are 3, 4, and 5, respectively, what is tan Z ?

    (A) 0.2
    (B) 0.6
    (C) 0.75
    (D) 0.8

Solution: Easy! SohCahToa! But first draw a picture. Recall from Skill 22, when a picture is described but not shown, draw it! The question asks for tan Z. Tan $= \dfrac{\text{opposite}}{\text{adjacent}}$. That means opposite leg over adjacent leg. So tan $Z = \dfrac{\text{opposite}}{\text{adjacent}} = \dfrac{3}{4} = 0.75$.

Correct answer: C

SAT Math Mantra #45
SohCahToa!

SohCahToa! Drills

Medium

1 Standing on Turtle's back, Vince casts a 4-meter shadow, as shown below. The angle of elevation from the tip of the shadow to the top of Vince's head is 40°. To the nearest tenth of a meter, how high is the top of Vince's head?

Ⓐ 1.6

Ⓑ 3.4

Ⓒ 5.5

Ⓓ 7.2

2 If $\sin A = \dfrac{3}{5}$, then which of the following could be $\tan A$?

Ⓐ $\dfrac{2}{5}$

Ⓑ $\dfrac{3}{4}$

Ⓒ 3

Ⓓ $\dfrac{5}{3}$

3 For right triangle $\triangle ABC$ with dimensions in feet as shown below, what is $\sin B$?

Ⓐ $\dfrac{5}{7}$

Ⓑ $\dfrac{2\sqrt{6}}{7}$

Ⓒ $\dfrac{2\sqrt{6}}{5}$

Ⓓ $\dfrac{7}{5}$

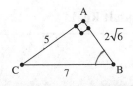

4 For right triangle XYZ shown below, what is $\cos Z$?

Ⓐ 0.2

Ⓑ 0.6

Ⓒ 0.75

Ⓓ 0.8

$$\mathrm{Cos}(x) = \sin(K - x)$$

5 In the equation above, the angle measures are in radians, and K is a constant. Which of the following could be the value of K?

Ⓐ $\dfrac{\pi}{4}$

Ⓑ $\dfrac{\pi}{2}$

Ⓒ π

Ⓓ 2π

Beyond SohCahToa

Half of the trig questions on the SAT are just SohCahToa, which you've now mastered. Many kids think that the rest of the trig questions are way beyond them, that you can only get them if you've had a full-year trig course. If you've had a trig course, that's great, and these questions will be especially easy for you. If not, the exciting news is that almost every trig question can be done with "Use the Answers" or "Make It Real"! You'll see examples of this when we review the Pretest question and in the drills.

Sometimes the SAT asks you to convert degrees to radians. To convert degrees to radians, multiply by $\frac{\pi}{180}$. For example, $30° \times \frac{\pi}{(180)} = \frac{\pi}{6}$ radians.

Lastly, occasionally the SAT has a question about the reciprocals of sin, cos, and tan, which are

$$\text{cosecant} = \frac{1}{\sin} = \frac{\text{hypotenuse}}{\text{opposite}} \qquad \text{secant} = \frac{1}{\cos} = \frac{\text{hypotenuse}}{\text{adjacent}}$$

$$\text{cotangent} = \frac{1}{\tan} = \frac{\text{adjacent}}{\text{opposite}}$$

Let's apply some of this to the question from the Pretest.

46. What is the value of θ, between 0 and 360, when sin θ = −1 ?

(A) 0
(B) 60
(C) 135
(D) 270

Solution: θ is just the symbol that people use for an angle when it's unknown. (The symbol is called *theta*.) Therefore, "what is the value of θ" means "what is the angle measure?" You probably could have guessed that anyway, since the question tells you that θ is between 0 and 360. Another example of "Don't get intimidated!" Just go with it, make an assumption on the SAT, and you'll probably be correct. They set it up that way. This is a great example of a Beyond SohCahToa question where you really don't need any trig. You just need to "Use the Answers"! Using your calculator, try each choice for θ, and see which one gives you sin θ = −1. Choice D is correct, because sin 270 = −1. If using the "sin" button is new for you, practice it right now. It's easy. Just hit "sin" and type "270" and hit Enter, and you'll get an answer of −1.

Correct answer: D

SAT Math Mantra #46
When trig seems tough, "Use the Answers" or "Make It Real."

Beyond SohCahToa Drills

Hard

1 What are the values of θ, between 0° and 360°, when tan θ = 1 ?

(A) 45°, 135 °, 225°, and 315°

(B) 45° and 135° only

(C) 45° and 225° only

(D) 45° and 315° only

2 Which of the following expressions gives the perimeter of the triangle shown below, with measurements as marked?

(Note: The law of sines states that the ratios between the length of the side opposite any angle and the sine of that angle are equal for all interior angles in the same triangle.)

(A) $59 + \dfrac{32 \sin 52}{\sin 74}$

(B) $59 + \dfrac{27 \sin 52}{\sin 74}$

(C) $59 + \dfrac{32 \sin 78}{\sin 54}$

(D) $59 + \dfrac{32 \sin 78}{\sin 52}$

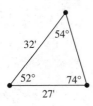

$Sec(x) = Csc(K - x)$

3 In the equation above, the angle measures are in radians, and K is a constant. Which of the following could be the value of K?

(A) 2π

(B) π

(C) $\dfrac{\pi}{2}$

(D) $\dfrac{\pi}{4}$

4 If b, c, and d represent positive real numbers, what is the minimum value of the function $f(x) = \sin b(x - c) - d$?

(A) 0

(B) 1

(C) $-1 - d$

(D) $d + c$

Directly and Inversely Proportional

This is something that you learned for maybe two classes, three years ago in Algebra I. But, for some reason, it's on the SAT. Weird, but here's the good news: it's super easy. In fact, it's an "easy" topic for us because as long as you know what's on this page, it's cake; the reason it's rated "medium" or "hard" is because most students don't know it.

"Directly proportional" means "x times some number gives you y."

For example, $y = 4x$ is "directly proportional" because 4 multiplied by each x yields each y value. The equation for directly proportional in general is $y = kx$. Sometimes the SAT also calls this "varies directly," as in "y varies directly with x." This is exactly the same as "directly proportional."

"Inversely proportional," on the other hand, means some number divided by x equals y.

This table shows an inverse proportion:

x	y
2	6
3	4
4	3
5	2.4
6	2

The equation for the relationship in the table is $y = \dfrac{12}{x}$, and the equation for inversely proportional, in general, is $y = \dfrac{k}{x}$. This also means that $xy = k$. In the SAT this is also called "inverse variation" or "varies inversely," as in "y varies inversely with x." Either way, it's the same.

Here's the question from the Pretest.

47. If y is directly proportional to x^3 and $y = 64$ when $x = 2$, what is x when $y = 216$?

Solution: "y is directly proportional to x^3" means $\dfrac{y}{x^3}$. So we set up a proportion between the two sets of (x, y) values and solve for the unknown x.

$$\frac{y}{x^3} = \frac{y}{x^3} \Rightarrow \frac{64}{2^3} = \frac{216}{x^3}$$ when you see a proportion, cross-multiply

$64x^3 = (8)(216)$ simplify (8)(216)

$64x^3 = 1728$ divide both sides by 64

$x^3 = 27$ take cube root of both sides

$x = 3$

Correct answer: 3

SAT Math Mantra #47

Directly Proportional means, "x times some number gives you y, so $y = kx$." Inversely proportional means "some number divided by x equals y, so $y = \dfrac{k}{x}$ or $xy = k$."

Directly and Inversely Proportional Drills

Medium

1 Which of the following expresses a relationship where y is directly proportional to x ?

Ⓐ

x	y
1	1
2	4
3	9
4	16

Ⓑ

x	y
1	5
2	10
3	15
4	20

Ⓒ

x	y
1	2
2	3
3	4
4	5

Ⓓ

x	y
1	2
2	6
3	12
4	16

2 If y is directly proportional to x^2, and $y = 18$ when $x = 3$, what is x when $y = 50$?

x	y
1	5
2	10
3	15
4	20

3 If y varies directly with x in the table above, what is the value of y when $x = 7.5$?

Ⓐ 30

Ⓑ 32.5

Ⓒ 35

Ⓓ 37.5

4 Which of the following expresses a relationship where y is inversely proportional to x ?

Ⓐ

x	y
1	1
2	4
3	9
4	16

Ⓑ

x	y
1	5
2	10
3	15
4	20

Ⓒ

x	y
2	54
3	36
4	27
6	18

Ⓓ

x	y
1	2
2	3
3	4
4	5

x	4	6	8	10
y	16	10.67	8	6.4

5 The table above gives values of a relation for selected values of x. Which of the following defines y in terms of x?

Ⓐ $y = 1.5x$

Ⓑ $y = x^{-1}$

Ⓒ $y = \dfrac{48}{x}$

Ⓓ $y = \dfrac{64}{x}$

Hard

6 If y is inversely proportional to x^2, and $y = 16$ when $x = 2$, what is x when $y = \dfrac{1}{2}$?

Ⓐ $8\sqrt{2}$

Ⓑ $4\sqrt{6}$

Ⓒ $\sqrt{2}$

Ⓓ 16

7 If y varies inversely with x and $y = 10$ when $x = 3$, what is the value of x when $y = 8$?

Ⓐ 1.75

Ⓑ 2.75

Ⓒ 3.75

Ⓓ 4.75

Remember how to add $\frac{3}{8}$ and $\frac{2}{9}$? You need a common denominator, so:

$$\frac{3}{8} + \frac{2}{9} = \frac{3(9)}{8(9)} + \frac{2(8)}{8(8)} + \frac{16}{72} = \frac{43}{72}.$$

When there is an x in the denominator (bottom) of the fraction, which is called a rational expression, it trips people out, but it's no different. We still just need to use a common denominator.

Let's look at the pretest question.

48. $\dfrac{3x+9}{x-3} + \dfrac{x+2}{x+3} =$

(A) $\dfrac{4x+11}{x^2-9}$ (B) $\dfrac{3x^2+121}{(x-3)(x+3)}$ (C) $\dfrac{4x^2+17x+21}{(x-3)(x+3)}$ (D) $\dfrac{4x^2+21}{x^2-9}$

Solution: Treat this just like the the arithmetic example above. We just need a common denominator, in this case $(x-3)(x+3)$, so:

$$\frac{3x+9}{x-3} + \frac{x+2}{x+3}$$

$$= \frac{(3x+9)(x+3)}{(x-3)(x+3)} + \frac{(x+2)(x-3)}{(x+3)(x-3)}$$

$$= \frac{3x^2 18x + 27}{(x-3)(x+3)} + \frac{x^2 - x - 6}{(x+3)(x-3)}$$

$$= \frac{4x^2 17x + 21}{(x-3)(x+3)}$$

Correct answer: C

SAT Math Mantra #48
When you see a variable in the denominator (bottom) of a fraction, get a common denominator.

Rational Expressions Drills

1 $\dfrac{3x+9}{x-3} + \dfrac{x+2}{x+3} =$

Ⓐ $\dfrac{4x+11}{x^2-9}$

Ⓑ $\dfrac{3x^2+121}{(x-3)(x+3)}$

Ⓒ $\dfrac{4x^2+17x+21}{(x-3)(x+3)}$

Ⓓ $\dfrac{4x^2+21}{x^2-9}$

2 For what values of x is the function

$f(x) = \dfrac{3x+9}{x-5} + \dfrac{x+2}{x+5}$ undefined?

Ⓐ 0 and 5

Ⓑ 5 and –5

Ⓒ 0, 5, and –5

Ⓓ There are no values for which the function is undefined

3 If m is an integer and a solution to the equation

$\dfrac{-2}{x-3} = \dfrac{2}{x+3} + \dfrac{1}{2}$, what is the value of m?

How to Think Like a Math Genius I

You've now learned the 48 skills that you need for the SAT. The Math Mantras remind you what to do when. In Skills 49 and 50, let's make sure you've memorized the 48 SAT Math Mantras. Cut out the flash cards provided at the end of this book, and drill them until you are ready to teach them. Then do that. Once you're sure you've got 'em, check off the box next to each mantra.

- [ ] **Skill 1.** When you see <u>variables</u> in the question and <u>numbers</u> in the answers, "Use the Answers."

- [ ] **Skill 2.** "What is m in terms of p and q" is just a fancy way of saying "solve for m" or "use algebra to get m alone."

- [ ] **Skill 3.** When you see the word "average" on the SAT, use sum = (average) × (number of items).

- [ ] **Skill 4.** When you see vertical angles, a linear pair, or a triangle, calculate the measures of all angles.

- [ ] **Skill 5.** When you see two parallel lines that are crossed by another line, eight angles are formed, and all the bigger-looking angles are equal, and all the smaller-looking angles are equal.

- [ ] **Skill 6.** When you see a triangle with two equal sides, mark the two opposite angles as equal, and when all sides of a triangle are equal, mark all angles 60°.

- [ ] **Skill 7.** An exterior angle equals the sum of the two far-away interior angles.

- [ ] **Skills 8 and 9.** Anytime you see a math vocab term, underline it.

- [ ] **Skill 10.** To solve a system of equations, use substitution or linear combination.

- [ ] **Skill 11.** The slope of a line measures its steepness; the steeper the line, the bigger the slope.

- [ ] **Skill 12.** Parallel lines have equal slopes, like $\frac{2}{3}$ and $\frac{2}{3}$. Perpendicular lines have negative reciprocal slopes, like $\frac{2}{3}$ and $-\frac{3}{2}$. And lines reflected over the x-axis or y-axis have negative slopes, like $\frac{2}{3}$ and $-\frac{2}{3}$.

- [ ] **Skill 13.** The key to understanding tables and graphs is to read the headings and the legend, if there is one.

- [ ] **Skill 14.** $f(3)$ means "plug 3 in for x."

- [ ] **Skill 15.** $f(m) = 9$ means "What did we plug into the equation for x to get a result of 9?"

- [ ] **Skill 16.** When you see <u>variables</u> in the question and <u>variables</u> in the answer choices, especially for word problems, use "Make It Real."

- [ ] **Skill 17.** The SAT only expects you to use formulas provided in the question or in the info box at the beginning of the section.

- [ ] **Skill 18.** The area of a donut equals the area of the big guy minus the area of the donut hole.

□ **Skill 19.** 4 boys to 5 girls could also be expressed 5 girls to 9 students. Also a ratio can be a reduced version of the real numbers.

□ **Skill 20.** When you see a proportion on the SAT, cross-multiply.

Here's the question from the Pretest.

Movie	Votes	
Superbad	♥ ♥ ♥ ♥ ♥	♥ = 10 votes
Borat	♥ ❨	
Wedding Crashers	♥ ❨	
Godfather	♥	

49. The table above shows the results of a survey in which 90 high school students voted for their favorite movie. Each student received one vote. According to the graph, how many more students favored *Superbad* than *Borat*?

(A) 3
(B) 3.5
(C) 35
(D) 39.5

Solution: The legend tells us that each ♥ represents 10 votes. Therefore, *Superbad* received 50 votes and *Borat* received 15, and 50 − 15 = 35. Remember that half a symbol represents 5 votes, not half a vote.

Correct answer: C

How to Think Like a Math Genius I Drills

Name the skill(s) that you can use, and then solve each question.

Easy

1 If $\dfrac{3}{12} = \dfrac{5}{a}$, what is the value of a?

Ⓐ 60
Ⓑ 40
Ⓒ 30
Ⓓ 20

2 If the average (arithmetic mean) of the perimeters of two shapes is 14, what is the sum of the perimeters of the two shapes?

Ⓐ 28
Ⓑ 21
Ⓒ 14
Ⓓ 7

Medium

3 If two sides of a triangle are equal, which of the following could be the measures of its angles?

Ⓐ 30, 30, 90
Ⓑ 35, 45, 100
Ⓒ 35, 35, 110
Ⓓ 30, 60, 90

4 Five boys on an elevator have an average (arithmetic mean) weight of 120 lb. A sixth boy wants to join them. If the elevator can hold 750 lb, what is the maximum the sixth boy can weigh in order for the group not to exceed the elevator's 750-lb weight limit?

5 If $f(x) = 3x^3$, and $f(b) = 24$, then $b =$

Ⓐ −1
Ⓑ 0
Ⓒ 2
Ⓓ 8

6 A fruit cup contains apple, pear, and banana in the ratio $2 : 3 : 4$. If a serving of a fruit cup contains 9 pieces of pear, how many total pieces of fruit are in the cup?

7 The function $M(u) = (2u)^2 - k$ expresses the number of songs Simon has memorized this year, where u represents months so far this year and $M(u)$ represents songs memorized. If by the end of June he has memorized 9 songs, what is the value of k?

Ⓐ 6
Ⓑ 9
Ⓒ 63
Ⓓ 135

Hard

8 If *a* is a multiple of 3 and *b* is a multiple of 4, which of the following must be a multiple of 12 ?

   I. ab
  II. $3a + 4b$
 III. $4a + 3b$

Ⓐ I only
Ⓑ III only
Ⓒ I and III
Ⓓ II and III

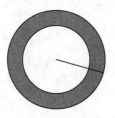

9 In the diagram above, what is the value of *a* in terms of *b* and *c* ?

Ⓐ $90 + 4b + c$
Ⓑ $180 - 3b - 2c$
Ⓒ $180 + 2b + c$
Ⓓ $360 - 4b - 2c$

10 The average (arithmetic mean) of the bowling scores of a team of *m* students is 170, and the average of the scores of a class of *n* students is 182. When the scores of both teams are combined, the average score is 177.5. What is the value of *m/n* ?

Ⓐ 0.4
Ⓑ 0.6
Ⓒ 0.8
Ⓓ 1

Learning Mantras is like learning martial arts. Practice until they become part of you, until you follow them naturally: when you see a proportion, you cross-multiply; when you see a linear pair, you fill in the angles. . . . This will fundamentally change you as a math student. In fact, after SAT prep, many students begin to like math; they realize that they "get" it, and it stops being intimidating, and becomes easy. I've even seen kids overcome serious math phobias with the Mantras. Your SAT score and probably even your math class grades will go way up.

Here are the rest of the SAT Math Mantras. Check the box next to each one when you have mastered it. Reread the Skill sections if you need to.

☐ **Skill 21.** "Use the Diagram" to estimate an answer. Translate into decimals any answer choices that contain $\sqrt{}$ or π.

☐ **Skill 22.** When a diagram is not drawn to scale, redraw it. And when a picture is described, but not shown, draw it!

☐ **Skill 23.** When you see a right triangle, try $a^2 + b^2 = c^2$.

☐ **Skill 24.** When you see a 30°, 45°, or 60° angle in a right triangle, try using the special right triangles.

☐ **Skill 25.** Similar triangles have sides that are proportional.

☐ **Skill 26.** Translate word problems from English to math.

☐ **Skill 27.** When something can be factored, FOILed, reduced, or simplified, . . . do it.

☐ **Skill 28.** Memorize the laws of exponents.

☐ **Skill 29.** Memorize these laws of exponents, too.

    1. $n^{-2} = n^{\frac{1}{2}}$ **2.** $2n^2 + n^2 = 3n^2$ **3.** $n^{\frac{3}{4}} = \sqrt[3]{n^4}$

☐ **Skill 30.** For the equation $y = mx + b$ or $y = ax + b$, m or a is the slope and b is the y intercept.

☐ **Skill 31.** SAT Math Mantra #31 When you see an arrangement question, draw a blank for each position, write in the number of possibilities to fill each position, and multiply. When an arrangement question mentions a "restriction," fill in the restricted positions first. When an arrangement question mentions a "team of two," divide your result by 2.

☐ **Skill 32.** Word problems are no-problem; translate English to math, plug numbers into the equation, and change fractions into decimals.

☐ **Skill 33.** When you see "probability," use the equation Probability $= \dfrac{\text{want}}{\text{total}}$.

☐ **Skill 34.** When you see "median," "mode," or "range," rewrite the data as a list in order , from lowest to highest.

☐ **Skill 35.** For the equation $y = ax^2 + bx + c$, the a tells whether the U-shaped graph opens up or down, and the c is the y-intercept. For the equation $y = (x - h)^2 + k$, the h and k give the coordinates of the vertex of the graph (h, k). The vertex is the highest or lowest point of the graph and is therefore also called the maximum or minimum point. For the equation $y = a(x - m)(x - n)$, m and n are the values of the x-intercepts, the places where the graph crosses the x-axi

☐ **Skill 36.** The equation for a circle is $(x - h)^2 + (y - k)^2 = r^2$, where (h, k) is the center and r is the radius of the circle.

☐ **Skill 37.** Remainders are what's left over when you use long division.

☐ **Skill 38.** When you see absolute value, look for the less obvious answer.

☐ **Skill 39.** An arithmetic sequence is a sequence of numbers where a certain number is ADDED to each term to arrive at the next, like 3, 7, 11, 15, 19. A geometric sequence is a sequence of numbers where a certain number is MULTIPLIED by each term to arrive at the next, like 3, –6, 12, –24, 48.

☐ **Skill 40.** The key to complex number questions is to treat i like a normal variable and then, in the final step, replace i^2 with –1.

☐ **Skill 41.** "Careless errors are bad mmmkay," so be fully present with each question: focused, relaxed, awake, and mindful. Oh, and also remember to distribute the negative: $-2(3x - 3) = -6x + 6$, not $-6x - 6$.

☐ **Skill 42.** "Careless errors are bad mmmkay," so underline all vocabulary words and remember to finish the question.

☐ **Skill 43.** Remember that small fractions multiplied by small fractions get smaller and that subtracting a negative number is like adding.

☐ **Skill 44.** Memorize the four types of transformation notation (up/down, left/right, thinner/thicker, reflection).

☐ **Skill 45.** SohCahToa!

☐ **Skill 46.** When trig seems tough, "Use the Answers" or "Make It Real."

☐ **Skill 47.** Directly Proportional means, "x times some number gives you y, so $y = kx$." Inversely proportional means "some number divided by x equals y, so $y = \dfrac{k}{x}$ or $xy = k$."

☐ **Skill 48.** When you see a variable in the denominator (bottom) of a fraction, get a common denominator.

Here's the question from the Pretest.

50. Ahmed is both the 7th tallest and 7th shortest student in class. If everyone is a different height, how many students total are in the class?

Solution: Draw a simple diagram. Anytime a picture or a situation is described, draw it (Skill 22). It helps you see what to do next and avoid careless errors. Without a diagram, many students answer 14 or 15, but the diagram shows that in height order, Ahmed is the 7th in both directions, so there are 6 students on each side of him. Thus, 6 students on his right plus 6 on the left plus Ahmed equals 13 students total.

Correct answer: 13

How to Think Like a Math Genius II Drills

Name the skill(s) that you can use, and then solve each question.

Easy

1 If $m < 0$, which of the following is greatest?

Ⓐ m

Ⓑ $3m$

Ⓒ $6m$

Ⓓ $9m$

2 If $p < -1$, which of the following is greatest?

Ⓐ p

Ⓑ $1 + p$

Ⓒ $1 - p$

Ⓓ p^3

3 If $m(x) = 2(3x)^2$, what is the value of $m(n)$?

Ⓐ $18\,n^2$

Ⓑ $36\,n^2$

Ⓒ $56\,n^2$

Ⓓ $72\,n^2$

Medium

4 If the Yoga Club has 42 members and the Dungeons and Dragons Live Action Role Playing Club has 25 members and there are 18 students who belong to both clubs, how many people total will be at a joint meeting of both clubs, if all members attend?

Ⓐ 18

Ⓑ 31

Ⓒ 49

Ⓓ 58

5 If 4 less than half a number is equal to 30 percent of the number, what is 3 times the number?

Ⓐ 12

Ⓑ 30

Ⓒ 60

Ⓓ 92

6 For the numbers in the data set {3, 5, 1, 7, 7, 3, 2, p, 1, 3,}, the median is 3 and the only mode is 3. Each of the following could be the value of p EXCEPT

Ⓐ 3

Ⓑ 4

Ⓒ 6

Ⓓ 7

Hard

7 Set M consists of m members, and set P consists of p members. And r represents the number of members that belong to both set M and set P. If set Z consists only of members who belong to either set M or set P, but not both, which of the following could represent the number of members of set Z ?

(A) $m + p - r$

(B) $m + p - 2r$

(C) $m - p - r$

(D) $m - p + 2r$

8 If each of the five finalists in the world SAT Math Olympics will face each of the others in head-to-head competition, how many of these one-on-one matches will be played?

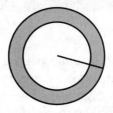

9 The dartboard shown above has a small circle, with radius 3.5, inside a larger circle, with radius 5. When Matty randomly throws a dart at the board, which of the following is closest to the probability that it will land in the shaded region?

(A) $\dfrac{1}{12}$

(B) $\dfrac{1}{6}$

(C) $\dfrac{1}{2}$

(D) $\dfrac{4}{3}$

10 If $|x - 3| = 4$ and $|y + 2| = 3$, what is the greatest possible value for $x - y$?

(A) 12

(B) 6

(C) −8

(D) −12

Brian's Friday Night Spiel: Recommendations for the Days Preceding the Test

Studies show that sleeping and eating healthfully two days before the test (or any important event) is as important as sleeping and eating healthfully the night before. So on Thursday night eat a healthy dinner and go to bed early—not so early that you're lying in bed at 7:00 p.m. tense, hungry, and staring at the cracks in the ceiling, but normal early, maybe 10:00 p.m.

Friday, have a normal day, no need to cram or stress. If you have completed this book and one or more timed practice tests, you are ready. Go to school, play sports or whatever you do after school, have a healthy dinner, and do something fun and relaxing. Don't hang out with anyone who stresses you out or obsesses over the test. Read, play a game, or watch a funny movie—I recommend *Fletch, Wedding Crashers,* or *40-Year-Old Virgin*—and go to bed at a sensible time. If you live in a household where, in the morning, everyone roams the house, screaming for a clean shirt and car keys, then gather your snack, drink, admission ticket, ID, pencils, watch, and calculator in the evening.

You should eat breakfast and pack a snack because it's a long day and you have to feed the brain. I recommend a cheese sandwich or two Luna bars, they are high in protein and not too high in sugar, good brain food. If you need an extra special boost, in India some people take a few drops of almond oil on the morning of a test.

Let's see if you got that.

Bonus Question

The night before the SAT you should

(A) Eat 2 pounds of pasta for a runner's endurance energy.

(B) Eat two whole live lobsters for omega-3 fatty acids.

(C) Host a huge pre-SAT party.

(D) Relax and sleep well.

Solution: Relax and sleep well, you are prepared. Now, go get 'em!
Correct answer: D

Test Day Checklist	
2 Protein bars	#2 Pencils
Beverage	Calculator
Your admission ticket	A watch (to keep track of time)
Photo ID (driver's license, school ID, or passport)	

Brian's Friday Night Spiel: Recommendations for the Days Preceding the Test Drills

Here is your last drill section. Your last assignment is to be able to stay relaxed, even under pressure. So here is a little tool that you can use anytime, even during the test.

In the 1970s Herbert Benson, a researcher at Harvard Medical School, published work on what he called the *relaxation response*, a physiological response where the body and mind relax. Benson reported that the relaxation response was triggered by practicing 20 minutes of a concentration exercise, basically meditation. Apparently, Yale, always in competition with Harvard, decided to one-up them. "We need a way to trigger the relaxation response but in less than Benson's 20 minutes!" they might have bemoaned. They researched, and they tried as hard as they could to relax; it was quite stressful. Finally, someone came up with the following goofy exercise. And it is goofy, but the thing is, it works! It totally works. Do it and you'll see.

Follow these steps:

1. Breathing through your nose, become aware of your breath.

2. Relax your shoulders and face.

3. Allow your exhale to be longer than your inhale.

4. Now, drop your shoulders and head and smile and then bring your head back up.

5. Repeat: drop your shoulders and head and smile, and then bring your head back up.

6. Notice how you feel.

That's it! Anytime you feel stressed, even during the test, try this very simple exercise to trigger your "relaxation response."

Score is tied: Yale, 1. Harvard, 1.

> Sucking all the marrow out of life doesn't mean choking on the bone.
> John Keating, *Dead Poets Society* (Touchstone Pictures, 1989)

Want to break 700? Here are the six steps to do it.

But first you have to promise me that you are doing this because you want to, and not out of some obsessive, sleep doesn't matter, gotta please my parents, if I don't go to Tufts I'm nothing, misunderstanding. Strive to do well, yes. Also stay balanced. Sleep. Eat well. Exercise. Be true to yourself. Be brave. Be honest. Be relaxed. Breathe. And from that place, give it all that you got . . . .

1 Make sure you understand all 50 Skills. Don't just look at them and say, "Yeah, I can do that." Practice. Do the drills. Make sure you can get every question correct on every Skill. If you can't, reread the section, read the solutions, and keep redoing the drills until they make perfect sense. Then teach them to a friend.

2 Memorize the careless errors to avoid. Keep them in mind as you drill until avoiding careless errors becomes second-nature.

3 Master Posttests I and II (Posttest II is available online at www.MH-SAT-TOP50-Math). Take each test, read the solutions, and redo any questions that you missed.

4 Once you've mastered Posttests I and II, take Posttest III (available online at www .MH-SAT-TOP50-Math), which consists of 50 very hard questions. Take the test, read the solutions, and redo any questions that you missed. When you master these 50 very challenging questions, you are ready to break 700!

5 Then take **at least** one timed SAT (see "Now What?" page 124). Score and review the test. Keep taking timed practice tests until you confidently and consistently break 700.

6 Finally, remember the words of quantum physics and of Jedi Master Yoda, "Do, or do not. There is no try." (*Star Wars Episode V: The Empire Strikes Back*, 20th Century Fox, 1980)

Let's revisit what I told you way back at the beginning of the book. It will probably make even more sense now.

In each math section of the SAT, the first third of the questions are "easy," the middle bunch are "medium," and a little less than the last third are "hard." In other words, of 30 questions, perhaps 10 are easy, 10 are medium, and 10 are hard. Both math sections are broken up into two parts, multiple choice and student-produced response, and each part is organized easiest to hardest.

Knowing this order of difficulty is important because you don't want to rush through the easiest and mediums just to get to the hard ones. All questions are worth the same amount. Not rushing is the best way to avoid careless errors. In school you might need to attempt all of the questions in order to do well, here you do not. **You only need to get to the very hardest questions if you are shooting for 700+.**

BUT, of course, since you lose no points for incorrect answers, you will put an answer for every question, even the ones you may not have time to look at. Keep track of time, and when there is a minute or two left, grid an answer for every question.

And, of course, now that you are a finely trained math ninja, if you are unsure of a question, take another look and ask yourself, "Which Math Mantra/Skill can I use?" Consider Make It Real, Use the Answers, and Use the Diagram, and if you're still stumped, do anything that you can. Can you factor, FOIL, reduce, simplify, translate, cross-multiply, or use the Pythagorean theorem? You don't need to see the whole plan in advance; just do whatever you can and it will help bring you to the next step. And, of course, use the process of elimination.

Now What?

Take the Posttest. Check your answers and review the Skills for any questions that were difficult. Then take Posttest II available online at www.MH-SAT-TOP50-Math. If you are shooting for 700+, take Posttest III (also available online at www.MH-SAT-TOP50-Math), which contains 50 "hard" questions.

After you have completed the Posttests, go to your guidance office and pick up the free packet entitled "SAT Preparation Booklet: Get Ready for the SAT," which contains a full practice test with answers and scoring instructions. Or you can download a free test at www.collegeboard.com.

Take the test as a dress rehearsal; get up early on a Saturday, time it, use the answer sheets, and fill in the ovals. If you have completed this book, you will find that you are very well prepared. Correct and score the test, and review whatever you got wrong. Figure out which SAT Math Mantras you could have used to get them right.

If you have some time, purchase *The Official SAT Study Guide*, published by The College Board. It contains additional official practice tests. Take one practice test per week as a dress rehearsal. Take it when you are relaxed and focused. We want only your best work. Less than that will earn you a lower score than you are capable of and is bad for morale. Score each test and review whatever you got wrong. Figure out which SAT Math Mantras you could have used to get them right.

Now, you are ready, you beautiful SAT monster. Go get 'em!

Posttest I

This posttest contains 50 questions that review our 50 Skills. Take the test. Then check your answers and review the Skills for any questions that were difficult.

 1 If $8^{x+1} = 2^{x+7}$, what is the value of x ?

(A) 1
(B) 2
(C) 3
(D) 4

2 If $2m = 5n$ and $5n = 6p$, what is m in terms of p?

(A) $5p$
(B) $3p$
(C) $2.9p$
(D) $2.4p$

3 On 10 tests, a student calculated her test average to be 82. However, she discovered that 2 of the grades were recorded incorrectly. The number 85 was entered as 80, and the number 99 was entered as 90. To the nearest whole number, what is the correct average for her 10 grades?

(A) 81
(B) 82
(C) 83
(D) 84

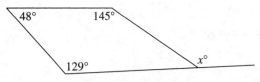

4 In the figure above, what is the value of x ?

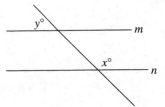

Note: Figure not drawn to scale.

5 In the figure above, $m \parallel n$. If $x = 53$, what is the value of y ?

(A) 27
(B) 53
(C) 90
(D) 127

Note: Figure not drawn to scale.

6 If $MN = ON$ in the figure above, and $b = 160$, what is the value of c ?

Ⓐ 5
Ⓑ 10
Ⓒ 20
Ⓓ 30

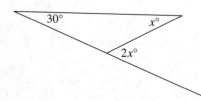

7 In the figure above, what is the value of x ?

$30° + x + 180 - 2x = 140°$

$30° - x$

$x = 30$

8 If three consecutive even numbers have a sum of 42, what is the smallest number?

9 If $12 < x < 36$, and 36 is the lowest number that is a multiple of 4, 12, and x, what is the value for x ?

$x + 3y = 12$
$3x - 3y = 8$

$x = 12 - 3y$

$36 - 45 - 3y = 8$

$-125 =$

$3y = -\frac{x}{3} + 4$

$3x - x - 12 = 8$

$2x$

10 What is the y-value of the solution to the system of equations above?

Ⓐ 4
Ⓑ $\dfrac{3}{7}$
Ⓒ $\dfrac{7}{3}$
Ⓓ 20

11 What is the slope of the line through the points (2, 3) and (−1, 0) ?

Ⓐ −1

Ⓑ 0

Ⓒ 1

Ⓓ 3

12 If the line through the points (−1, 3) and (−2, p) is parallel to the line $y = 3x − 3$, what is the value of p ?

Ⓐ −2

Ⓑ −1

Ⓒ 0

Ⓓ 1

Spice Girl	Votes
Scary	♥ ♥ ♥ ♥ ♥
Baby	♥ ♥
Ginger	♥ ♥
Posh	♥ ♥ ♥
Sporty	♥ ♥ ♥ ♥

♥ = 20 votes

13 The table above shows the results of a survey in which 310 high school students voted for their favorite Spice Girl. Each student received one vote. According to the graph, how many more students favored Scary Spice than Posh Spice?

Ⓐ 1.5

Ⓑ 15

Ⓒ 20

Ⓓ 30

14 If $f(x) = −3x^2 − 2$, what is the value of $f(−1)$?

Ⓐ −6

Ⓑ −5

Ⓒ 1

Ⓓ 5

x	$f(x)$
0	2
1	3
2	6
3	11

15 The table above shows the values of the quadratic function f for selected values of x. Which of the following defines f ?

Ⓐ $f(x) = x^2 + 1$

Ⓑ $f(x) = x^2 + 2$

Ⓒ $f(x) = 3x^2 − 2$

Ⓓ $f(x) = 3x^2 − 1$

16 If t is a negative number, which of the following must be a positive number?

Ⓐ $t + 1$

Ⓑ $t + 2$

Ⓒ $3 − t$

Ⓓ $\dfrac{t}{3}$

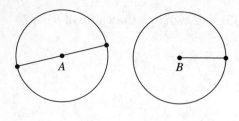

Note: Figure not drawn to scale.

17 For the circles above, the diameter of circle *A* is 16 and the radius of circle *B* is half the diameter of circle *A*. What is the area of circle *B* ?

Ⓐ 8

Ⓑ 16π

Ⓒ 24π

Ⓓ 64π

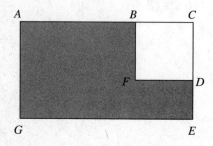

18 In the figure above, the perimeter of square *BCDF* is 24, *DE* = 4, and *AB* = 12. What is the perimeter of the shaded region?

Ⓐ 28

Ⓑ 43

Ⓒ 56

Ⓓ 68

19 The ratio 1.4 to 2 is equal to which of the following?

Ⓐ 1 to 4

Ⓑ 14 to 2

Ⓒ 10 to 7

Ⓓ 7 to 10

20 A scale model of a certain airplane is $\frac{3}{35}$ the height of the actual airplane. If the scale is 3.5 inches tall, what is the height of the actual plane?

Ⓐ 38 $\frac{4}{5}$

Ⓑ 40

Ⓒ 40 $\frac{5}{6}$

Ⓓ 42

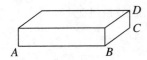

21 The rectangular solid above has edges of length 20, 8, and 4. If point M (not shown) is the midpoint of segment AB, what is the length of MD ?

(A) $4\sqrt{2}$

(B) $3\sqrt{10}$

(C) $6\sqrt{5}$

(D) $2\sqrt{65}$

22 $ABED$ is a square with sides of length 6. If point C is the midpoint of ED, what is the perimeter of $ABCD$?

(A) 18

(B) $15 + 3\sqrt{5}$

(C) $18 + 3\sqrt{5}$

(D) $22 + 3\sqrt{5}$

Note: Figure not drawn to scale.

23 In the right triangle above, what is the value of p?

(A) 8

(B) 16

(C) 32

(D) 48

24 In right triangle MNO (not shown), the measure of MN is 6 and the measure of NO is 3. Which of the following could be the measure of OM ?

(A) 3

(B) $3\sqrt{3}$

(C) $4\sqrt{3}$

(D) $5\sqrt{3}$

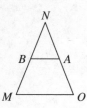

25 In the isosceles triangle *MNO* above, a segment is drawn between midpoints *A* and *B* of the two congruent sides. All the following are true EXCEPT

Ⓐ $\angle M \cong \angle O$

Ⓑ $\angle B \cong \angle A$

Ⓒ $\triangle MNO \sim \triangle BNA$

Ⓓ $BA = MO$

26 When the product of 3 and a number is increased by 5, the result is 350. What is the number?

27 If $x = p(p - 3)$, then $x + 2 =$

Ⓐ $p^2 - 3p$

Ⓑ $p^2 + 3$

Ⓒ $p^2 - 3p + 2$

Ⓓ $p^2 + 3p + 2$

28 What is the product of $3bm^4$ and $2b^4$?

Ⓐ $5mb^8$

Ⓑ $6mb^8$

Ⓒ $6m^4b^4$

Ⓓ $6m^4b^5$

29 If $a^{-3} = b^{-9}$, what is the value of *a* when $b = 2$?

Ⓐ -2

Ⓑ 0

Ⓒ 8

Ⓓ 16

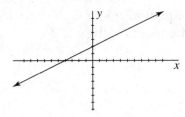

30 The figure above shows the graph of the line $y = ax + b$. Which of the following best represents the graph of $y = 3ax + b$?

Ⓐ
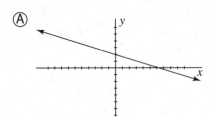

Ⓑ
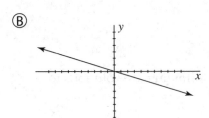

Ⓒ
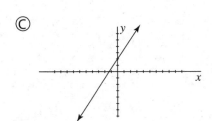

Ⓓ
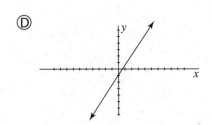

31 For a fundraiser, the yoga club is selling tee-shirts with a choice of two slogans, "Ooom-mmm" or "Bend me!" Each shirt is available in lavender or peach and in small, medium, or large. How many different types of shirts are available?

32 A researcher estimates that the population of an ant colony is growing at a daily rate of 0.7%. If the current population of the colony is 10,000 ants, which of the following expressions approximately models the population of the ant colony t days from now according to the researcher's estimate?

Ⓐ $10{,}000(1 - 0.007)^t$

Ⓑ $10{,}000(1 + 0.007)^t$

Ⓒ $10{,}000 - 1.007^t$

Ⓓ $10{,}000(0.007)^t$

33 What is the probability of randomly choosing a prime number from the set 1, 4, 5, 6, 7, 8?

34 If $2m - 2$, $m + 3$, and $3m - 4$ are all integers and $m + 3$ is the median of these integers, which of the following could be a value for m?

Ⓐ 2

Ⓑ 4

Ⓒ 6

Ⓓ 8

35 If m is a positive constant and $n = 0$, which of the following could be the graph of $y = mx^2 + 3x + n$?

Ⓐ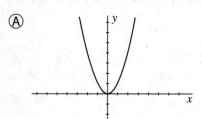

Ⓑ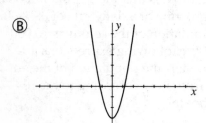

Ⓒ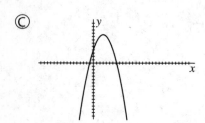

Ⓓ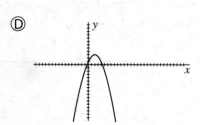

36 The graph of the equation $x^2 + 4x + y^2 - 2y = 4$ is a circle. What is the radius of the circle?

37 Which of the following could be the remainders when four consecutive odd integers are each divided by 3 ?

Ⓐ 1, 3, 5, 0

Ⓑ 1, 2, 3, 4

Ⓒ 0, 1, 2, 3

Ⓓ 0, 2, 1, 0

38 Which of the following are solutions to $|x - 2| = 6$?

I. 8

II. −4

III. −3

Ⓐ I only

Ⓑ II only

Ⓒ I and II

Ⓓ I and III

$$6, 10, 18, 34, \ldots$$

39 In the sequence above, the first term is 6, and every number after the first is found by subtracting 1 and then doubling the result. What is the 7*th* term in the sequence?

Ⓐ 257

Ⓑ 258

Ⓒ 259

Ⓓ 260

40 What is the square of the complex number $(i - 3)$?

Ⓐ 2

Ⓑ 8

Ⓒ $8 - 6i$

Ⓓ $10 - 6i$

41 When $x = -2$, which of the following is equivalent to $x(2s^2 - 2)$?

Ⓐ $-4s^2 + 4$

Ⓑ $-4s^2 - 4$

Ⓒ $4s^2 - 4$

Ⓓ $4s^2 + 4$

42 If $x = 2$, then which of the following is equivalent to $(y - x)^2$?

Ⓐ $y - 2$

Ⓑ $y^2 + 4$

Ⓒ $y^2 - 4y + 4$

Ⓓ $y^2 + 4y + 4$

$N \qquad -4$

43 If point N on the number line above represents -8, and point M (not shown) is between N and -4, which of the following could be represented by point M ?

Ⓐ 8

Ⓑ 4

Ⓒ 0

Ⓓ -5

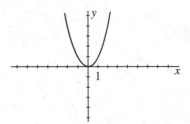

44 The graph of $g(x)$ is shown above. Which of the following equations represents all the points of $g(x)$ shifted 1 unit down?

Ⓐ $y = g(x) + 1$

Ⓑ $y = g(x + 1)$

Ⓒ $y = g(x - 1)$

Ⓓ $y = g(x) - 1$

45 If two angles of a triangle measure 40° and 110°, what is the measure of the third angle in radians?

46 For what value of θ, between 0° and 180°, does sec θ = 2 ?

Ⓐ 30°

Ⓑ 45°

Ⓒ 60°

Ⓓ 90°

47 If y is inversely proportional to x^2, and $y = \dfrac{1}{2}$ when $x = 2$, what is x when $y = \dfrac{1}{8}$?

Ⓐ 4

Ⓑ 2

Ⓒ $\sqrt{5}$

Ⓓ $\sqrt{8}$

48 For what value of x is the function $f(x) = \dfrac{x^4 - 81}{x - 25}$ undefined?

49 In a basket of orange and purple crayons, the ratio of orange crayons to purple crayons is 2 to 3. Which of the following could be the total number of crayons in the basket?

Ⓐ 2

Ⓑ 6

Ⓒ 14

Ⓓ 15

$\{4, 5, 6, 7, 8, 9\}$

50 What is the probability of randomly choosing an odd prime number from the set above?

BONUS QUESTION

The morning of the test you should

Ⓐ Drink 4 Jolt colas to be wide awake.

Ⓑ Feed your brain with a tall stack of flapjacks, a side of pork, and six potatoes.

Ⓒ Run a few miles.

Ⓓ Have a normal healthy breakfast.

Solutions

Pretest

Solutions are on each Skill page.

Skill 1 (page 11)

Use the Answers

1. **C** You can answer this question quickly and easily by using simple algebra and solving for x. If, however, that is difficult or daunting, "Use the Answers." Just plug each choice in to see which one makes the equation work. Choice C is correct: $2(10) - 3 = 17$.

2. **D** You can answer this question, like #1 above, by using algebra and solving for p. Or you can just "Use the Answers." Plug each choice in to see which one makes the equation work. Choice D is correct: $4(3) + 2 < 15$.

3. **C** You can answer this question by using algebra and solving for j, or just "Use the Answers." Plug each choice in to see which one makes the equation work. Choice C is correct: $\frac{3+1}{2^3} = \frac{4}{8} = \frac{1}{2}$.

4. **D** You can answer this question by using algebra and solving for n, or just "Use the Answers." Plug each choice in to see which one makes the equation work. Choice D is correct: $|3 - 6|$ equals 3 which is less than 4. ($|3 - 6|$ means the absolute value of $3 - 6$, which is just fancy language for subtract $3 - 6$ and make the answer positive. More on this in Skill 38).

5. **A** You can answer this question by using algebra and solving for t; however, this "medium" difficulty question requires more involved algebra. "Use the Answers" makes the question EASY! Just plug each choice in to see which one makes the equation work. Choice A is correct since $\sqrt{\frac{-2(-54)}{3}} = \sqrt{\frac{108}{3}} = \sqrt{36} = 6$.

6. **D** "Use the Answers" makes this easy. Just plug the choices in for u in the equation. Each choice yields a result (which represents production cost) less than $7300. So 4 is the highest and thus the correct answer. This question is rated "hard" because it involves functions, fractions, and variables in the exponents; difficult for many students, but easy for you with "Use the Answers."

Skill 2 (page 13)

"What Is p in Terms of f?"

1. **D** "What is R in terms of D and T?" means "solve for R." In other words, get R alone.

   $D = RT$ divide both sides by T

   $\frac{D}{T} = R$

2. **B** "What is m in terms of p?" means "solve for m, get m alone." Since $3m = 2n = 4p$, we can say
   $3m = 4p$ divide both sides by 3

   $m = \frac{4p}{3}$

3. **B** "What is $b - 1$ in terms of x and k?" means solve for $b - 1$, get it alone. This is unusual. Your math teacher never asks for $b - 1$, she just asks for b. But the SAT is weird and asks for $b - 1$. So we simply solve for $b - 1$, no biggie.

   $x + 3(b - 1) = k$ subtract x from both sides

   $3(b - 1) = k - x$ divide both sides by 3

   $b - 1 = \frac{k - x}{3}$

4. **D** "What does p^{-1} equal in terms of q?" means solve for p^{-1}. Your math teacher would never ask you to solve for p^{-1}, but the SAT does. No problem, just solve for p^{-1}, get it alone.

   $5p^3q^{-2} = 25p^2$ divide both sides by p^2

   $5pq^{-2} = 25$ divide both sides by $5q^{-2}$

   $p = \frac{5}{q^{-2}} 5q^2$ the question asks for p^{-1}, so just bring both sides to the $^{-1}$ power, that is, take the reciprocal of both sides

   $p^{-1} = \frac{1}{5q^2}$

5. **B** Don't get intimidated by this word problem. Most of the words in the question actually just define the variables. We just need to algebraically manipulate the equation to get p alone:

$$L = \sqrt{2x}\,\frac{p}{5q^2} \qquad \text{multiply both sides by } 5q^2$$

$$5q^2\,L = \sqrt{2xp} \qquad \text{divide both sides by } \sqrt{2x}$$

$$\frac{5q^2L}{\sqrt{2x}} = p$$

Skill 3 (page 15)

"Mean" Means Average

1. **D** Set up the average formula: $(m + 4m)/2 = 30$. Then use algebra to solve for m or "Use the Answers" to see which one works.

2. **B** Most kids get this one wrong, but with the sum formula it's easy! Set up the sum formula: Sum = $(k)(21)$. Therefore, Sum = $21k$. EASY!

3. **D** Set up the sum formula: $(m + n) = 7 \times 2$. Thus, $m + n$ equals 14. Then use the sum formula for the second set of data: $(m + n + p) = 11 \times 3$. So their sum is 33. Since $m + n + p$ equals 33 and $m + n$ equals 14, p must equal $33 - 14 = 19$.

4. **D** This question is a medium because many people fear fractions. Don't! They are easy, you can even turn them into decimals on your calculator if you don't like them (just divide the top number by the bottom number). With the average formula this question is very easy. Average = sum / number of items. So average = $9/2$.

5. **C** Set up the sum formula to find the sum for each class, then add the sums and divide by the total number of students in the classes to arrive at the combined average:

$$\frac{(80)(20) + (92)(30)}{30 + 20} = 87.2$$

6. **130** This question follows our strategy perfectly. If the average of m, n, o, and p is 55, then their sum is $55 \times 4 = 220$; and if m, n, o, p, and q average to 70, then their sum is $70 \times 5 = 350$.

Therefore the value of q is the difference between the sums: $350 - 220 = 130$.

7. **25** If five judges average 7, then using our sum formula, sum = average × number of items, the sum is 35. If we want one judge's number to be as big as possible, then we want the other judges' numbers to be as low as possible. Since they must be "different integers," the first four numbers would be 1, 2, 3, 4, which are the lowest different positive integers. These numbers add up to 10, so we have $35 - 10 = 25$. The last judge can give a whopping score of 25.

Skill 4 (page 17)

The 6-Minute Abs of Geometry: Angles

1. **C** As soon as you see a linear pair of angles, determine the measure of the unknown angle in the pair. So the angle next to 153° must be $180 - 153 = 27°$. Now we have two of three angles in a triangle which must add up to 180, so the third must be $180 - 80 - 27 = 73$.

2. **B** This is essentially the same question as #1 above. But notice that this figure is not drawn to scale. Whenever this happens, just redraw it roughly to scale. This one is very easy. The angle next to 80° must be $180 - 80 = 100$. Now we have two of three angles in a triangle which must add up to 180°, so the third must be $180 - 100 - 25 = 55$.

3. **C** Mark $y = 60$ into the figure, and as soon as you see a linear pair, solve the other angle, which in this case equals $180 - 60 = 120$. Now we have four of the five angles of a five-sided figure. A five-sided figure has 540°, so 540 minus the other angles equals the measure of angle z.
$z = 540 - 120 - 133 - 139 - 64 = 84$.

4. **30** Use the smaller triangle to determine x ($2x + 75 + 45 = 180$, so $x = 30$). Then use x to solve for the angles in the other triangle:

$120 + 30 + z = 180$

$150 + z = 180$

$z = 30$

5. D The two angles form a linear pair, so $2m + 3n = 180$. We need "n in terms of m," so we use algebra to solve for n:

$2m + 3n = 180$ subtract $2m$

$3n = 180 - 2m$ divide by 3

$n = \dfrac{180 - 2m}{3}$

Skill 5 (page 19)

The 6-Minute Abs of Geometry: Parallel Lines

1. C Easy! In a pair of parallel lines there are only two kinds of angles, big and little, and the two add up to 180. Since $y = 45$, $x = 180 - 45 = 135$.

2. D Parallel lines cut by a transversal make two kinds of angles, big and little. Clearly x is little and z is big. If $x = 66$, then $z = 180 - 66 = 114$.

3. A First, mark the info that is given in the question into the diagram. That always helps make the question simpler and usually shows which of our geometry strategies to use. Then use vertical angles, linear pairs, triangles, etc. to calculate the measures of any other angles that you can. The vertical angle to z is 40, and the linear pair to x is 50, so now we have two angles of the triangle. $180 - 50 - 40 = 90$, so the linear pair of y is 90 and therefore $y = 180 - 90 = 90$.

4. B Mark the info from the question into the diagram. Then mark all other angles that you can determine. Now x and y are a linear pair, so $x + y = 180$ and $x = 180 - 95 = 85$. Since the figure is not drawn to scale, you can resketch it to scale. When you do this, you notice that if z and x are both less than 90, the lines cannot be parallel—they are heading toward each other and will intersect. Only choice B is true.

5. D Use the strategies. Mark $x = 22$. Therefore, in the triangle, the missing angle is $180 - 108 - 22 = 50$. And in the pair of parallel lines y is a big, not a little, angle; thus it equals $180 - 50 = 130$.

Skill 6 (page 21)

The 6-Minute Abs of Geometry: Triangles

1. D As soon as you see an equilateral triangle, mark each angle 60°. Then since r forms a linear pair with 60° angle UEQ, $r = 180 - 60 = 120$.

2. B As soon as you know that two sides in a triangle are equal, you know that the two angles opposite the two sides are also equal. Therefore, $a = c$. Now $b = 43$, and $a + c + 43 = 180$, so $a + c = 137$. Since a equals c, c is half of 137, which equals 68.5.

3. D Mark info from the question into the diagram. Since $AC = AB = 7$ and the perimeter is 21, CB must also equal 7 and the triangle is equilateral. Therefore, all angles of the triangle are 60°.

4. C Area = 0.5(base)(height)

$72 = 0.5(12)(MN)$

So $MN = 12$ and the triangle is isosceles. Therefore, the base angles are equal. Since angle M is 90°, the base angles must add up to $180 - 90 = 90$, and since they are equal, they are 45° each.

Skill 7 (page 23)

The Final 6-Minute Abs of Geometry

1. 90 We've seen this question before, but now we have even more Skills to answer it. Look for our strategies. Are there vertical angles we can use? No. Linear pairs? Maybe. Triangles? Shaboom! $2x + 75 + 45 = 180$, use algebra to get $x = 30$, and plug that into the other triangle. So $30 + 30 + y = 180$. Use algebra to get $y = 120$. Also Skill 7 gives us a shortcut here since y is an exterior angle to the first triangle and must equal $45 + 75$. So, $y - x = 120 - 30 = 90$.

2. 125 First, label all info that is given in the question into the diagram. Since the measure of $\angle AEB$ is 70, $\angle DEC$ must also be 70 since they are vertical angles. Then $\angle BEC$ makes a linear pair with $\angle AEB$ and must be $180 - 70 = 110$. If segment EF (not shown) bisects $\angle BEC$, then $\angle FEC$ is 55, half of 110. So $\angle FED$ equals $55 + 70 = 125$.

3. Ⓓ The vertical angle of x in the triangle is 71, so the other two angles of the triangle add up to $180 - 71 = 109$. Each of these angles makes a linear pair with y and z, respectively. So these two angles plus y and z make two linear pairs and equal $2(180)$. Therefore, $109 + y + z = 360$. So use algebra to get $y + z$ alone. In math class this would be unusual. You teacher usually wants you to solve for just y or just z, but sometimes the SAT asks for $y + z$, so we solve for that. No problem. $y + z = 360 - 109 = 251$.

4. Ⓐ The dotted lines form a small triangle inside the larger triangle. Since the dotted lines bisect angles x and y, the angles of this triangle are

$z, \dfrac{1}{2}y, \dfrac{1}{2}x$. So $z + \dfrac{1}{2}y + \dfrac{1}{2}x = 180$ "What is the

value of z?" means solve for z. So

$z = 180 - \dfrac{1}{2}y - \dfrac{1}{2}x$ .This does not initially seem

to match any answers, but $180 - \dfrac{1}{2}y - \dfrac{1}{2}x =$

$180 - 0.5\,(x + y)$.

Skill 8 (page 25)

Math Vocab

1. ⑤ This question simply tests whether you know the words "consecutive" and "integer." Many students do not and wind up intimidated and they skip this very easy question. Since you know what these two words mean, use simple trial and error to solve this question.
$4 + 5 = 9$.

2. Ⓒ Most people know that since $3^2 = 9$, there is at least one answer to this question. But the term "different" is the keyword here. It is the tipoff that perhaps there is more than one answer. That should be enough to jog your brain to realize that $(-3)^2 = 9$ also. So there are two possible answers to the question, 3 and -3.

3. Ⓓ Lots of students don't know the term "units digit" and get this wrong; since you know, it's easy. Just list the possibilities: 3, 13, 23, 33, 43, 53, 63, 73, 83, 93.

4. ③① This question intimidates many people. I know so many students who would immediately say, "I have no chance," and move on. I

think that this is something the SAT is testing: can you be intimidated? Shout with me now, "NO WAY!" So once we're done with that, this is easy. Just list a bunch of prime numbers: 2, 3, 5, 7, 9, 11, 13, 17, 19, 23, 29, 31 and look for two in a row (consecutive) that add up to 60. So $29 + 31 = 60$. Cake, if you stay relaxed, focused, and confident.

5. Ⓒ Probably best to just find the two numbers. If that seems difficult, "Use the Answers" for hints, that is try -12 and -14. The two numbers are indeed -12 and -14, so I and III are true. II is a trick that the SAT tried and that we can totally predict. -12 might seem less than -14, since 12 is less than 14, but the bigger the negative number, the smaller it is; like the more you owe, the bigger the debt. This sort of trick is discussed more in Skill 43.

6. Ⓒ There are two conditions that make a mathematical expression undefined: taking the square root of a negative number and dividing by zero, so $\sqrt{2x-5}$ is undefined if $2x - 5 < 0$ (i.e., if it is negative). So simply solve the inequality:

$2x - 5 < 0$

$2x < 5$

$x < \dfrac{5}{2}$ makes the expression undefined.

You could also "Use the Answers" and try values from each answer choice to see which one produces a negative inside the square root.

7. Ⓒ There are two conditions that make a mathematical expression undefined: taking the square root of a negative number and dividing

by zero, so $\dfrac{2x}{(x-3)(x+4)}$ is undefined when

$(x - 3)$ or $(x + 4)$ equals zero. Simply solve $x - 3 = 0$ and $x + 4 = 0$ to get $x = 3$ and $x = -4$. Notice that 0 is not a solution since plugging 0 in for x does not actually produce a 0 in the denominator (bottom) of the fraction.

Skill 9 (page 27)

More Math Vocab
Answer to Brian's Math Magic Trick #1—Multiples:
You said carrot. Impressed?

1. **A** List the factors of 120, or better yet "Use the Answers." Just divide 120 by each answer choice. If the number goes into 120 evenly (without a remainder), then it is a factor. And 7 is not a factor, since $120 \div 7 = 17.14$.

2. **D** This question tests if you know the terms "odd" and "factor." Once you do, this is a simple "Use the Answers" type question. Try each answer. Choice A does not work because 2 is not an odd number. To test each of the other choices, simply divide 114 by the number. If it goes in evenly, which means you get an integer (no decimal or fraction), then it is a factor. For example, $114 \div 55 = 2.07$, and therefore 55 is not a factor of 114. Choice D is correct since $114 \div 57 = 2$.

3. **D** This question simply asks you to factor 48 and count how many factors there are. To factor a number, make a list of pairs, as shown below. When you reach 6×8, you know that you have them all since only 7, which does not go into 48, is between 6 and 8. Finding factors systematically like this is far

   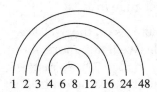

   1 2 3 4 6 8 12 16 24 48

   better than randomly jotting down numbers. This is true for any SAT math question. Systematic and organized is better than scattered and random. It avoids careless errors, allows you to look back at your work, and helps you make the leap to the next step needed on a complicated question.

4. **B** To complete this question, we factor 48 just as we did above. However, this time we circle any prime numbers in the list. The numbers 2 and 3 are the only prime numbers in the list. Then we write the list of the factors for 100: 1, 2, 4, 5, 10, 20, 25, 50, 100. Of the prime factors of 48, only 2 is also a factor of 100. So set P has one member.

5. **D** This question could be difficult, but "Use the Answers" makes it easy! Just test each answer choice by dividing it by 10, 12, and 15. Now 60 is the lowest number on the list that is divisible by 10, 12, and 15. Notice that several other answers work also, but 60 is the lowest.

Make sure to finish the question and try all choices!

6. **C** Just try numbers for a, b, and c. This is called "Make It Real" and is discussed more in Skill 16. Let's say $a = 3$, $b = 5$, and $c = 7$. Then $ab^2c = (3)(5)^2(7) = 525$. The long way to do this question is to list the factors of 525: 1, 3, 5, 7, 15, 21, 25, 35, 75, 105, 175, 525. The shortcut is to notice that since a, b, and c are prime, the factors will be 1, a, b, c, ab, ac, bc, b^2, ab^2, cb^2, abc, and ab^2c.

Skill 10 (page 29)

Systems of Equations

1. **A** You can use substitution or linear combination, but substitution will be easier. Solve the first equation for y by dividing both sides of the equation by 3 to get $y = 4 + 2x$. Then plug $4 + 2x$ into the second equation for y to get:

   $3x + 4(4 + 2x) = 60$

   $3x + 16 + 8x = 60$

   $11x + 16 = 60$

   $11x = 44$

   $x = 4$

2. **B** For this system, linear combination is easier. Add the equations, and the y terms cancel, leaving $5x = 20$, so $x = 4$. Plug $x = 4$ into either equation and solve for y:

   $2(4) + 3y = 12$

   $8 + 3y = 12$

   $3y = 4$

   $y = \dfrac{4}{3}$

   CARELESS ERROR BUSTER: Notice that choice A is the answer for the value of x, but the question asks for the value of y. Make sure to finish the question; before choosing an answer, ask yourself, "Did I finish the question, and did I answer the question asked?"

3. **D** When you solve this system of equations, you get something like $0 = 0$, which means the two equations are equivalent—there are two

forms of the same line, and there are infinitely many solutions. You can also see that if you multiply the second equation by 3, you get the first equation.

4. Ⓑ For the system to have no solutions, the lines must never intersect. So they must be parallel and therefore have the same slope. Solve both equations for $y = mx + b$, m representing the slope. The slope of the first is $\frac{2}{3}$ and the slope of the second is $\frac{n}{6}$, so $\frac{2}{3} = \frac{n}{6}$ and $n = 4$.

5. Ⓒ Don't be intimidated by a long word problem. Convert the words into math. If we call the number of chocolate chip cookies C and the number of servings of crème brûlée B, we get:

$1.50C + 4.50B = 120$

$C + B = 50$

Use substitution to get:

$75 - 1.5B + 4.50B = 120$

$75 + 3B = 120$

$3B = 45$

$B = 15$

6. Ⓒ Solve both equations for y and sketch a graph. To make $(0,0)$ a solution, the value for a must be less than b. You can also "Use the Answers" and test each answer choice to see which makes $(0, 0)$ a solution.

Skill 11 (page 31)

Slaloming Slope I

1. Ⓑ Plug the two points into the slope equation.

$$\frac{y - y}{x - x} = \frac{-4 - a}{-2 - 3} = \frac{-4 - a}{-5} = \frac{3}{5}$$

Once you have $\frac{-4 - a}{-5} = \frac{3}{5}$, you can simply "Use the Answers" and try each answer choice to see which one makes the equation work. You could also cross-multiply (see Skill 20).

2. Ⓑ This question is exactly like Question 1. You are given two points, and you simply plug them

into the slope formula. The only twist is that the question refers to the origin as one of the two points so you have to know that "origin" means $(0, 0)$, which is just vocab. Know it (which you do now) and you get it correct!

$$\frac{y - y}{x - x} = \frac{-3 - 0}{2 - 0} = \frac{-3}{2}$$

Notice how $\frac{-3}{2}$ is not a choice. Don't be thrown. Be confident, unshakeable! After you finish this book, you will always know what to do; don't let the question intimidate you. So, which choice matches our $\frac{-3}{2}$? Just enter it in your calculator, remember that $\frac{-3}{2}$ means "-3 divided by 2," and you get -1.5. Bingo!

3. Ⓒ Use two points to count the $\frac{\text{rise}}{\text{run}}$, the change in y over the change in x.

4. Ⓒ Remember that pictures on the SAT are drawn exactly to scale (we'll talk more about this excellent strategy in Skill 21). So just use the picture to determine the values of (a, b); it looks like $(4, 4)$. The question just asks for $\frac{b}{a}$, so the answer is choice C, since $\frac{4}{4} = 1$.

5. Ⓑ To get the slope of MN, we must know the coordinates for M and for N. Since these points are centers of the circles, they are halfway between the endpoints of each diameter shown. So M equals $(2, 1)$ and N equals $(7, 3)$. Now we plug these into the slope formula.

$$\frac{1 - 3}{2 - 7} = \frac{-2}{-5} = \frac{2}{5}$$

Skill 12 (page 33)

Slaloming Slope II

1. Ⓐ Plug the two points into the slope equation.

$$\frac{0 - 3}{-1 - 2} = \frac{-3}{-3} = 1 \text{ Since we want the line to be}$$

perpendicular, take the negative reciprocal, -1.

2. **D** Parallel lines have equal slopes. The slope of line $y = -2x - 3$ is -2 (which we will review in Skill 30), so the slope of the two points given is

$$\frac{-3 - p}{4 - 2} = -2 \text{ "Use the Answers" or cross-multiply}$$

(see Skill 20) to solve for p. $p = -7$.

3. **B** The origin means $(0, 0)$. Plug the two points into the slope equation.

$$\frac{-3 - 0}{2 - 0} = -\frac{3}{2}$$

Since we want the slope of a line perpendicular, we take the negative reciprocal, which is $\frac{2}{3}$.

4. **D** This question is quite difficult for most students. But with our strategies it's very easy. We know that two lines that are reflections of each other have slopes with opposite signs, so instead of $\frac{2}{3}$, line n has a slope of $-\frac{2}{3}$.

5. **C** Use the slope formula to solve for b. Then use the value of b in the slope formula for the second pair of points, and solve for m. Because the lines are parallel, the second pair also has a slope equal to 1.

Skill 13 (page 35)

Using Tables, Bar Graphs, and Pie Graphs

1. **C** Test each choice. Choice I is correct since i represents the total of $c + f$, which is the total of $a + b + d + e$. That is why II is also correct. Choice III, however, is false since $g + c$ does not equal i.

2. **275** Since Sra. Moran and Mrs. Nicholas received the most votes, they must represent the 30% and 25% sections which are largest. These add up to 55%. Since there were 500 students surveyed, we want 55% of 500 which means $0.55 \times 500 = 275$.

3. **D** Use the graph to estimate sales for each book. Then add those up and divide by 4 to get the average. Notice that the graph tells us that the numbers represent thousands of books! So the answer is choice D. Remember, the key to tables and graphs is to read the headings and legend, if there is one.

4. **A** This is an unusual graph, but one that the SAT uses quite often. If it seems difficult, work with it until it makes sense. The coordinates of each point represent the student's score on the two tests. So we are looking for a point where the y value (test II) is bigger than the x value (test I). Even though we cannot determine exact values on the graph, point A $(70, 90)$ clearly has the largest increase from test I to test II. Point B improves less $(70, 80)$, and the other three choices went down from test I to test II.

Skill 14 (page 37)

Function Questions on the SAT, Type I

1. **A** Simply plug -2 in for x in the equation.

$$f(-2) = 2(-2)^3 - 2 = -18.$$

2. **D** The long way to solve this question is to plug (5) and (-5) into each equation in the answer choices to see which one makes $f(5) < f(-5)$. This absolutely works and is worth the time since it will earn you points. There is also a faster way. In every other answer choice, 5 plugged in for x will clearly give the same or higher value than when -5 is plugged in. However, choice D, $f(x) = 2 - x^3$, is the only one where a positive number yields a lower result than a negative: $2 - 5^3 < 2 - (-5)^3 \Rightarrow -123 < 127$.

3. **D** This is a very common SAT question. Just choose an (x, y) point from the table and see which equation works. Choice D is correct since $11 = 3(2)^2 - 1$. Try all equations, in case several work. Then you would just choose a second point to find the one answer choice that works for both points.

4. **D** This is a very typical SAT question, appearing on nearly every SAT. If you got this question wrong and you spend the time to master it, you will gain points! In this question, you are given values for the number of cars, which is x, and for pints of soap, which is $g(x)$. $g(x) = 140$ and $x = 3$. Simply plug these values in for x and $g(x)$, and use basic algebra to solve for k. If this is confusing, redo this question over and over until you can teach it to a friend. Then do that! This is a great party question. Next

time you go to a party, bring this one, people love it. OK, I'm kidding.

$$g(x) = 5x - (4x + k)$$
$$3 = 5(140) - (4(140) + k)$$
$$3 = 700 - 560 - k$$
$$3 = 140 - k$$
$$-137 = -k$$
$$137 = k$$

5. **B** Plug 3 into the h function to get 15 and then plug that result, 15, into the m function to get 255.

$$h(3) = 2(3)^2 - 3 = 15$$
$$m(15) = (15)^2 + 2(15) = 255$$

6. **C** Plug 2 in for x in the g function to get $g(2) = f(2) + 2$. Since $f(2) = 2(2) + 3 = 7$, we get $g(2) = 7 + 2 = 9$.

7. **C** $f(3)$ means "plug 3 in for x" and get y. Usually we use an equation to answer this, but in this question we use the graph shown. We simply locate $x = 3$ on the graph and see what the y value is at that point. $y = -2$. Then the question asks for $f(-2)$, so we look on the graph once again, but this time we plug -2 in for x.

The best answer is $y = -\dfrac{11}{3}$.

Skill 15 (page 39)

Function Questions on the SAT, Type II

1. **C** This question asks you if $f(m)$ equals -3, what is m? To solve, simply plug m in for x and -3 for the result: $-3 = 2(m)^2 - 3$. Then use algebra to solve for m, or "Use the Answers."

2. **D** Simply plug a in for x and -39 in for $f(x)$. Then solve for a. This question has one additional part. Once you know the value of the variable a, you have to plug that value in for the a in $4 - 2a$ to get $4 - 2(-2) = 4 + 4 = 8$.

3. **B** This question asks when $y = 2$ on the graph, what is the value of x? Look on the graph at the y values. There are two points on the graph where $y = 2$. These two points occur at $x = 4$ or $x = -4$. Since $x = 4$ is not a choice, choice B is the answer.

4. **A** Plug $(p - 1)$ in for n in the $m(n)$ function.

$$m(p - 1) = (p - 1)^2 + (p - 1) = p^2 - 2p + 1 + p - 1 = p^2 - p$$ which matches choice A: $h(p) = p^2 - p$.

5. **38** People hate this question, but once you know the trick, it's easy! For $3h(v) = 54$, just use basic algebra and divide both sides by 3 to get $h(v)$ alone; $h(v) = 18$. Now, this is just a type II question—you are given the result and you must find v. Plug v in for x and 18 in for $h(x)$: $v - 2 = 18$, so $v = 20$. Cake! Last step: the question did not ask for v, that might have made it "medium" difficulty. It asks for one more step. Once you know the value of v, the question asks for $h(2v)$. Easy, $h(2v) = h(2 \cdot 20) = h(40) = 40 - 2 = 38$. I know, this question asks a lot; it's definitely a "hard," but if you stay focused and use these tools, you can get it.

6. **0** $g(3m) = 3g(m)$ means $(3m)^2 - 3 = 3(m^2 - 3)$. Use algebra to solve for m.

$$(3m)^2 - 3 = 3(m^2 - 3)$$
$$9m^2 - 3 = 3m^2 - 9$$
$$6m^2 = -6$$
$$m^2 = -1$$

Since m is a real number, m^2 cannot equal -1, so there are zero solutions.

Skill 16 (page 41)

Make It Real

1. **C** This question intimidates some students; it seems too theoretical. But "Make It Real" makes it so easy. Just choose a real number for p (remember that the question says that the number that you choose has to be even). Let's say $p = 4$. Then try $p = 4$ in all the answer choices to see which one does what the question asks, which one gives us an even number. The answer is choice C since $2(4) - 2 = 2$.

2. **B** "Make It Real." Let's say $x = 5$ and $n = 1$. Now it's easy, "5 days ago Striped was born and she is now 1 day older than Yellow." So Striped is 5 days old and 1 day older than Yellow, who must therefore be 4 days old. When we plug our numbers, $x = 5$ and $n = 1$, into each answer choice, the one that gives 4 is correct. Choice B is correct, $5 - 1 = 4$.

3. **C** Easy, choose a number for p, let's say $p = -3$. (Notice the question states that p must be negative. Underline that vocab word!) Now use

your calculator to solve $(5 \times 10^{-3}) + (1 \times 10^{-3}) =$ 0.006. Remember to use the order of operations. Whichever choice yields 0.006 is correct. Choice C is correct, $6(10)^{-3} = 0.006$.

4. **D** Let's say $q = 5$. Now just follow the directions. $5 \times 7 = 35$. $35 + 7 = 42$. $42/7 = 6$. When $q = 5$, the answer is 6. So plug 5 in for q in the answer choices; whichever one equals 6 is correct. Choice D is correct, $5 + 1 = 6$.

5. **D** We are into the "hards" now. But "Make It Real" will knock these down a notch to mediums or even easies. Still, since they are "hards," we may have to try several different numbers to find the one right answer. In this question, m can be any number between −2 and 5, and n can be any number between −1 and 2. Let's choose a few possibilities and see which choice always works.
If $m = -2$ and $n = -1$, $mn = 2$.
If $m = 5$ and $n = 2$, $mn = 10$, so since it can be as high as 10, choices A and B can be eliminated.
If $m = -2$ and $n = 2$, $mn = -2$.
If $m = 5$ and $n = -2$, $mn = -5$.
So, choice D is the only answer that includes all the possibilities. Notice that the best way to determine all the possibilities is to use the most extreme values for each interval and multiply them.

6. **C** So easy with "Make It Real!" Let's say $n = -0.5$. Then $n^2 = 0.25$ and $n^3 = -0.125$. n^2 is the greatest since it is the only positive number, and n is the least, so C is correct.

7. **A** Let's say $a = 3$ and $v = 4$. Then

$$m = \frac{3a^2}{v} = \frac{3(3)^2}{4} = \frac{3(9)}{4} = \frac{27}{4} = 6.75$$

If a and v are doubled, then $a = 6$ and $b = 8$ and

$$m = \frac{3a^2}{v} = \frac{3(6)^2}{8} = \frac{3(36)}{8} = \frac{108}{8} = 13.5$$

Since 13.5 is double 6.75, the answer is choice A.

Skill 17 (page 43)

Perimeter, Area, Volume

1. **A** The perimeter of the rectangle is $7 + 7 + 3 + 3 = 20$. Since the square has four equal sides and its perimeter is also 20, each side must be $20 \div 4 = 5$.

2. **B** Since the radius of circle B is half the diameter of circle A, it must be 5. Therefore, the area of circle B is $a = \pi r^2 = \pi(5^2) = 25\pi$.

3. **C** The surface area equals the addition of the faces. There are three square faces (area $= m$) and two triangular faces (area $= n$), so the total surface area $= 3m + 2n$.

4. **C** Since volume $=$ length $\times$ width $\times$ height, just determine the volume for each part of the block. The smaller part $= 5 \times 1 \times 1 = 5$, and the larger part $= 5 \times 3 \times 1 = 15$. So the volume of the whole block $= 5 + 15 = 20$.

Skill 18 (page 45)

Donuts

1. **C** If the perimeter of square $BCDF$ is 24, each side is 6 and the area is 36. The area of $ACEG$ is $A = (l)(w) = (18)(10) = 180$. So the area of the shaded region is $180 - 36 = 144$.

2. **A** The area of the larger circle is $A = \pi r^2 = \pi(8)^2 = 64\pi$. The radius of the smaller circle is half the radius of the larger circle. So the area of the smaller circle is $A = \pi r^2 = \pi(4)^2 = 16\pi$. The area of the unshaded region is $64\pi - 16\pi = 48\pi$.

3. **39** Fun question. Remember that the area of a shaded region equals area of big guy minus area of donut hole. The area of the whole rectangle is $6 \times 9 = 54$, and the area of the unshaded triangle is (this is the cool part) $a = 0.5bh = 0.5(5)(6) = 15$. It looks like the height wasn't given, but it is; it's 6, it's as tall as the rectangle. So the shaded region $= 54 - 15 = 39$.

4. **9** Since the triangles are similar, their sides are proportional (more on this in Skill 25).

Therefore, $\dfrac{AD}{ED} = \dfrac{BD}{CD}$ and $\dfrac{4}{2} = \dfrac{6}{CD}$, so $CD = 3$. (How would you know to set this up? You'll see that Mantra 25 says, "Similar triangles have sides that are proportional," so when the SAT says "similar," that's what they want you to set up. That's how to think like a math genius!) The area of the larger triangle is $0.5(\text{base})(\text{height}) = 0.5(4)(6) = 12$, and the area of the smaller triangle is $0.5(\text{base})(\text{height}) = 0.5(2)(3) = 3$. So the area of the shaded region is $12 - 3 = 9$.

Skill 19 (page 47)

Baking Granola Bars . . . Ratios

1. **B** When the SAT says the ratio of carrots to potatoes is 2 to 7, that can be the actual numbers of carrots and potatoes or a reduced version of the actual numbers. For example, instead of 2 : 7 it could be 4 : 14 or 6 : 21 or any multiple of 2 : 7. Therefore, the top number, which represents carrots, must be a multiple of 2.

2. **C** When the SAT says that 2 out of 5 are pears, that can be the actual numbers of pears or a reduced version of the actual numbers. Since 2 out of 5 are pears, 3 out of 5 are apples, and the actual number of apples must be a multiple of 3.

3. $\frac{2}{3}$ or 0.666 or 0.667 "Fraction" is a synonym for "ratio"—they mean the same thing. So we just want the ratio of questions that are not true/false to total questions. Out of 60 questions, 20 were true/false, so 40 were not true/false questions. Thus, the ratio (aka fraction) of not true/false to total is 40 : 60 or $\frac{2}{3}$.

4. **D** The measures of the angles must add up to 180°. Obviously 1 : 3 : 5 does not add up to 180, so multiply all three by the same number until we get 180. $1 : 3 : 5 \Rightarrow 2 : 6 : 10 \Rightarrow 10 : 30 : 50 \Rightarrow 20 : 60 : 100$. That adds up to 180, so the smallest angle is 20°.

5. **B** This question uses the same process as Question 4 with one extra step. Once you know the angles, just subtract the smallest from the largest: $100 - 20 = 80$. Some students get this wrong because they do not finish it; they see the choices 20 or 100 and choose one. This is a great careless error to practice avoiding (Skill 42).

6. **4.8** You are given the ratio of pretzels to corn chips but are asked for the ratio of pretzels to total mixture. So switch it to pretzels to total. There are 3 ounces of pretzels per 7 ounces of corn chips, so there are 10 ounces total ($3 + 7 = 10$). The ratio of pretzels to total is

3 to 10. Thus, $\frac{3}{10} = \frac{p}{16}$.

When you see a proportion, cross-multiply. $p = 4.8$.

Skill 20 (page 49)

More Granola Bars . . . Proportions and Cross-Multiplying

1. **C** Just set up the proportion. $\frac{15}{50} = \frac{x}{1}$.

   Remember to set it up so that flour is on top in both ratios. If does not actually matter if it's on top or bottom, just that it is in the same spot in both. Then cross-multiply and solve for x.

   $(15)(1) = (50)(x)$ divide both sides by 50 $x = 0.3$.

2. **A** Without our cross-multiplying technology this question could be quite vexing. But cross-multiply and it's easy. Pretty much anytime you see a proportion, cross-multiply. $mn = 60$.

3. **D** Cross-multiply. $mn = 36m$. To solve for n, divide both sides by m so you get $n = 36$.

4. **D** Let's convert $\frac{1}{4}$ into a decimal (just divide 1 by 4, which equals 0.25) and set up the proportion.

   $\frac{0.25}{4} = \frac{1.5}{x}$.

   Cross-multiply and simply solve for x. $6 = 0.25x$, so $x = 24$.

5. **D** Without cross-multiplying, this question would be difficult. However, just cross-multiply each answer choice. All are equal ($mp = on$), except choice D ($mn = op$).

Skill 21 (page 51)

Use the Diagram

1. **B** First, draw point A into the diagram; always draw any info from the question into the diagram. Since $NA = AO$, point A is in the middle (the midpoint) of NO. Using the diagram, you can then see that if MO equals 12, MA must be less, but not 6, which would be only half of 12. So the only answer that can work is 9.

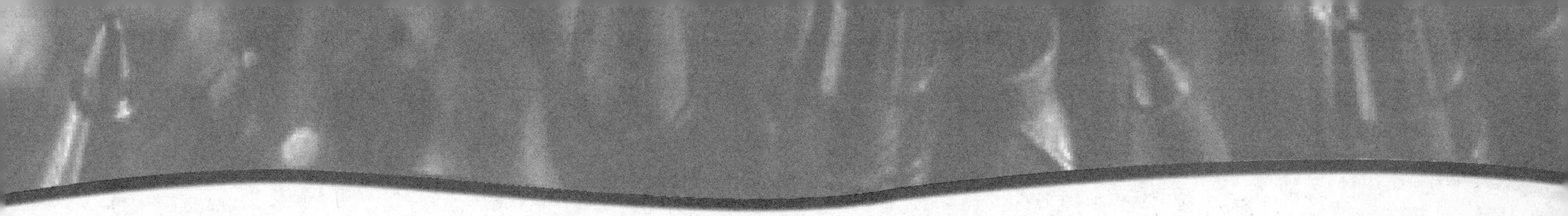

2. Ⓓ I will show you the exact geometry for a question like this in Skill 23, but for now, here's the "Use the Diagram" shortcut. First, draw *M* into the diagram. Then just estimate its length and translate each of the answers into decimals and choose the one closest to your estimate.

3. Ⓐ Easy. The radius of the large circle is 6, so the diameter is 12. Use this to estimate the perimeter of the weirdly shaped unshaded region. Then translate each answer from *p* to decimals and see which one is closest to your estimate. This strategy works so well because usually the answer choices are far enough apart that our estimate works.

4. Ⓐ Draw *JM* and based on *LK*, estimate its length. If we say *LK* = 1, then *JM* seems to be approximately 1.8. So the ratio is 1/1.8 = 0.555. Translate the answer choices to decimals and choice A is closest.

Skill 22 (page 53)

Art Class

1. Ⓓ Draw a diagram. Since *N* is between *M* and *O*, *LN* must be longer than 12 and shorter than 24. Only choice D is a possibility.

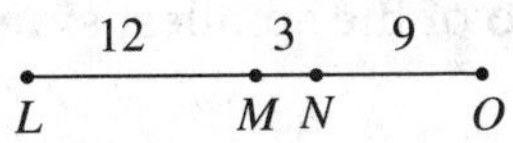

$$\overset{\displaystyle 12 \qquad 3 \quad 9}{\underset{\textstyle L \qquad\quad M\ N \qquad O}{\rule{5cm}{0.4pt}}}$$

2. **3 or 7** Without a sketch, this is tough; with a diagram, it's easy. *b* can be 3 or 7.

3. Ⓒ When you redraw to scale, often the answer becomes obvious. With all sides equal and ∠*AGE* = 90°, *AE* is slightly longer than *CE*. So the ratio of *AE* to *CE* = approximately 1.5 to 1. Translate the answers to decimals, and only choice C is close to 1.5. You could also use special right triangles (Skill 24).

4. Ⓐ Draw a diagram. The diagram shows that the segment must be less than 2, perhaps 1.5. Convert the answers to decimals and only choices A and B are possible. The answer is choice A because the segment forms a special right triangle with sides 1, 1, and $\sqrt{2}$ (another preview of Skill 24).

5. Ⓒ Redraw to scale; *KL* should be drawn a little shorter to make it 4 (a third of *LN*). Then using

lengths that we are given as a key, we estimate *JM*, which is clearly a little more than 12. So only choices C and D are possible, and choice D is likely. This is an awesome strategy; we eliminated two choices on a "hard" question. The correct answer is choice C. To get an exact answer, we need, once again, special right triangles. Let's hear it for Skill 24, on the way!

Skill 23 (page 55)

The 6-Minute Abs of Geometry: Length of a Side I

1. Ⓒ Anytime you see a right triangle on the SAT, try $a^2 + b^2 = c^2$. Also, for any question with a diagram, mark info from the question into the diagram. Here *m* and *n* are the short sides, and *o* is the longest (also called the hypotenuse), so $5^2 + 12^2 = o^2$, so $169 = o^2$ and *o* = 13.

2. **15** Here 8 and *p* are the short sides (the longest side is always opposite the right angle). So

$$8^2 + p^2 = 17^2$$
$$64 + p^2 = 289$$
$$p^2 = 225$$
$$p = 15.$$

3. Ⓑ When a picture is described but not shown, draw a diagram. This helps you visualize and organize the info and shows you what to do next. The question does not state whether 10 is another short side like 4 or if it is the longest side. But we can "Use the Answers." Simply try each answer choice along with 10 and 4 in $a^2 + b^2 = c^2$, always using the biggest number for *c*. To make that easier, convert all the choices to decimals. Choice A is not correct

since $4^2 + (2\sqrt{19})^2 \neq 10^2$. Choice B is correct

since $4^2 + (2\sqrt{21})^2 = 10^2$.

4. **15** When a picture is described, but not shown, draw a diagram. This helps you visualize and organize the info and shows you what to do next. Once we see the diagram, piece of cake. We know the hypotenuse is 13, and we see that the length of one side is 5, so $5^2 + b^2 = 13^2$. Use algebra to get *b* = 12. But now don't forget to finish. The length of *b* is 12, so *m* = 12 + 3 = 15.

5. (A) If the longest side is x and the lengths of the sides are consecutive integers, then the shorter sides can be called $(x - 1)$ and $(x - 2)$. Now, we just plug these into $a^2 + b^2 = c^2$ to get $(x - 2)^2 + (x - 1)^2 = x^2$.

Skill 24 (page 57)

The 6-Minute Abs of Geometry: Length of a Side II

1. (A) When a picture is described but not shown, draw a diagram. This helps you visualize and organize the info and shows you what to do next. The question does not state whether 8 is another short side like 4 or if it is the longest side. But we can "Use the Answers." Simply try each answer choice in $a^2 + b^2 = c^2$, always using the biggest number for c. Choice I is not correct since $4^2 + 4^2 \neq 8^2$, choice II is correct since $4^2 + 4\sqrt{3}^2 = 8^2$, and choice III is not correct since $4^2 + 2^2 \neq 8^2$.

2. (C) As soon as you see a right triangle with a 60° angle, use the special right triangle 30, 60, 90. The hypotenuse is 12, so the smallest leg must be 6. A triangle congruent to the one shown will also have a shortest leg of 6, since they are congruent.

3. (B) An isosceles right triangle is a right triangle where two sides are the same length. When two sides are equal (great review from Skill 6), their two opposite angles are also equal. Therefore, we have a 90, 45, 45 triangle. Since the two equal sides add up to 6, each is 3, and the longest side is $3\sqrt{2}$.

4. (D) In Skill 22, we redrew the diagram to scale and estimated the answer. With special right triangles we can get the exact answer. As soon as you see a right triangle with a 30° angle, use the special right triangle 30, 60, 90. We are given the longest side $LN = 10$, so the side opposite the 30° angle is 5 and LM is $5\sqrt{3}$. Similarly, since $KL = 6$, $KJ = 3$ and $JL = 3\sqrt{3}$. Thus, $JM = 5\sqrt{3} + 3\sqrt{3} = 8\sqrt{3}$.

Skill 25 (page 59)

The 6-Minute Abs of Geometry: Length of a Side III

1. (B) Triangle ABC is isosceles, so $AB = BC$. Similar triangles have proportional sides, so

$$\frac{BC}{NO} = \frac{AC}{MO} \Rightarrow \frac{4}{6} = \frac{3}{MO}.$$

When you see a proportion, cross-multiply, so $4MO = 18$, and $MO = 4.5$.

2. (B) When a picture is described but not shown, draw it. Fill in the sides of special right triangle PQR: 3, $3\sqrt{3}$, 6. The sides of similar triangle MNO must be proportional to the sides of PQR, so the sides of MNO must be multiples of 3, $3\sqrt{3}$, 6. Choice B is correct since 6, $6\sqrt{3}$, $12 = 2(3, 3\sqrt{3}, 6)$.

3. (D) When you see a right triangle, try $a^2 + b^2 = c^2$. Based on the diagram, $3^2 + b^2 = 5^2$, so $b = 4$. Then when a picture is described but not shown, draw it. Draw PRQ and fill in the sides of both triangles. Since the triangles are similar, their sides are proportional. The ratio of the small side of one triangle to the small side of the other is given as 2 or 2 : 1, so the lengths of all the sides of the pictured triangle are twice those of triangle PRQ. Thus, the perimeter, which is 12, of the triangle shown must be twice the perimeter of PRQ, which is therefore 6.

4. (A) Similar triangles have proportional sides. We are told that the ratio between the sides is 3 : 5. Therefore, the ratio of the smallest sides is

$$\frac{x}{4} = \frac{3}{5}.$$

Skill 26 (page 63)

"Is" Means Equals . . . Translation

1. (C) This is direct translation. Product means multiply and sum means add, so $(b)(2) =$

$$b + \frac{2}{3} \text{ or } 2b = b + \frac{2}{3}$$

2. (B) Each foot has 12 inches, so f feet has $12f$ inches, and c inches is just c inches, so there is a total of $12f + c$.

3. (D) Translate and solve. $p + 6 = 5p$, so $p = 1.5$. Then remember that the question did not ask for p—it asked for $8p$, so simply multiply $8(1.5) = 12$. This is a great careless error to learn to avoid; many students lose points by forgetting to finish the question. This is normal, since your math teacher always asks for p, not $8p$. But, now you know to expect this on the SAT, and you won't lose points.

4. **46.30** Nona paid 8% sales tax, so the original price can be found with the equation: $(P)(1.08) = \$50$.

$$P = \frac{50}{1.08} = 46.296 = 46.30.$$

The question asks you to round to the nearest cent, so $46.296 = 46.30$.

5. **$\frac{2}{3}$, 0.666, or 0.667** Translate: $2x + 3y = 1.20(5y)$.

Normally in school you solve for x or y. This question asks you to solve for $\frac{y}{x}$. No biggie, just manipulate the equation to get $\frac{y}{x}$ on one side.

$2x + 3y = 1.20(5y)$
$2x + 3y = 6y$
$2x = 3y$
$\frac{2}{3} = \frac{y}{x}$.

6. **(A)** Translate and solve for m. $(m + 11)^2 = (m + 1)^2 (9)$. To simplify, take the square root of both sides to eliminate the squares to get

$m + 11 = (m + 1)(3)$
$m + 11 = 3m + 3$
$8 = 2m$
$4 = m$
You could also "Use the Answers."

Skill 27 (page 65)

Just Do It! . . . Springboard

1. **(D)** Classic springboard. If you see a fraction that can be reduced, do it. So $\frac{3}{18} = \frac{1}{6} = \frac{a}{k}$, so k could equal 6.

2. **(D)** If you see something that can be multiplied, do it. $p(p + 2) = p^2 + 2p$, so $m = p^2 + 2p$. To find $m - 3$, we just subtract 3 from both sides to get $m - 3 = p^2 + 2p - 3$.

3. **12** If you see $x^2 - y^2$, factor it, so $(x - y)(x + y) = 108$, and we are told that $(x + y) = 9$, so $9(x - y) = 108$, and $(x - y) = 12$.

4. **(B)** If something can be FOILed, do it. $(x + n)(x + 1) = x^2 + 1x + nx + n$. Since that also equals $x^2 + mx + 5$, we know that $n = 5$, and therefore $m = 1 + 5 = 6$.

5. **(C)** If you see something that can be simplified, do it.

$$12\sqrt{12} = 12\sqrt{4 \cdot 3} = 12 \cdot 2\sqrt{3} = 24\sqrt{3}$$

So $p = 24$ and $q = 3$ and $\frac{p}{q} = 8$.

6. **(B)** If something can be FOILed, do it. $(x - 3y)^2 = (x - 3y)(x - 3y) = x^2 - 6xy + 9y^2$. Since $xy = 11$, $x^2 = 5$, and $y^2 = 7$, we have all the parts and $x^2 - 6xy + 9y^2 = 5 - 6(11) + 9(7) = 2$.

Skill 28 (page 67)

Beyond Your Dear Aunt Sally:
The Laws of Exponents I

1. **(A)** When you multiply variables, like x, you add the exponents, so $(x^2)(2x^3) = 2x^5$.

2. **(C)** $(3m^4)(2b^4) = 6m^4b^4 = 6(mb)^4$. Notice that this time I did not add the exponents because m and b are different letters, and we only add when the letters are the same.

3. **(A)** Great "Use the Answers" review. Since there are variables in the question and numbers in the answer choices, we can try the answers. The question asks for the greatest value of b, so we'll start with the biggest choice, 5. Plugging 5 in for b in the question, we get $2^a \cdot 2^5 = 64$. $2^5 = 32$, so $2^a \cdot 32 = 64$. Divide both sides by 32 to get $2^a = 2$, which could work if $a = 1$. Thus, 5 works for b and is the largest choice.

4. **(D)** Great vocab review; underline "different positive integers." Often, noticing and remembering to apply these words is the key to the question. Also great "Use the Answers" review. Since there are variables in the question and numbers in the answer choices, we can try the answers. The question asks for the greatest value of p, so we'll start with the biggest choice, 5. Since we want p to be as big as possible, we'll make m and n as low as possible, 1 and 2, since they need to be "different positive integers." Plug 5 in for p in the question; we get $2^1 \cdot 2^2 \cdot$

$2^5 = 128$. Trying $p = 4$, we get $2^1 \cdot 2^2 \cdot 2^4 \neq 128$, which works.

5. **A** For $p^m \cdot p^6 = p^{12}$, we add the exponents, so $m = 6$. For $(p^3)^n = p^{21}$, we multiply the exponents, so $n = 7$. So $n - m = 1$.

6. **A** "What is the value of b in terms of a?" means solve for b, get b alone. To get b alone and eliminate the exponent, we take the eighth root of each side ($\sqrt[8]{}$), since $\sqrt[8]{b}$ is the opposite of b^8. So, taking the $\sqrt[8]{}$ of both sides, we get $\sqrt[8]{a^4} = a^{1/2} = b$. We will deal with this more in Skill 29.

Skill 29 (page 69)

Far Beyond Your Dear Aunt Sally:
The Laws of Exponents II

1. **C** $2x^2$ and $2x^3$ are not like terms and do not combine. To combine, the variable (x) and the exponents would have to match.

2. **B** Since both terms have an x^2, they are like terms. To add them, we add their coefficients. "Coefficient" is the fancy vocab term for the number in front of the variable. So $4x^2 + 5x^2 = 9x^2$.

3. **A** To multiply $3m^{-2}$ by $2m^{-5}$, we add the exponents, so $(3m^{-2})(2m^{-5}) = 6m^{-7} = \dfrac{6}{m^7}$.

4. **D** Great question! $3^{n/p}$ means $\sqrt[p]{3^n}$. So $\sqrt[p]{3^n} = \sqrt{27}$. And $3^n = 27$, so $n = 3$ and $p = 2$. So $(n)(p) = (3)(2) = 6$.

5. **D** For $p^m \cdot p^{-4} = p^5$, we add the exponents, so $m = 9$. For $(p^{-2})^n = p^{20}$, we multiply the exponents, so $n = -10$. So $n - m = -10 - 9 = -19$.

6. **C** Somehow, we need to get 243^{-1}, meaning we need to get $\dfrac{1}{243}$ using 3s. This should stir you to play with your calculator and arrive at $3^5 = 243$ and $3^{-5} \dfrac{1}{243}$. So $m + n + p = -5$. Since they all must be negative numbers, they can be $-1, -2, -2$ or $-1, -1, -3$. So $nmp = -4$ or -3.

Skill 30 (page 71)

Your Algebra Teacher Never Said "$y = ax + b$"

1. **C** 25 people are offended by each joke, so that number goes next to x. 50 people are

offended right off the bat, and this number does not change with the number of outrageous jokes in the movie, so that number goes alone. $y = 25x + 50$.

2. **−1** If you are given a point and an equation, plug in the point and solve for the unknown:
$$y = -2x + 3$$
$$g = -2(2) + 3$$
$$g = -1.$$

3. **D** If you are given a point and an equation, plug in the point and solve for the unknown. So plug (2,1) into $y = mx - 2$ to get $m = \dfrac{3}{2}$. Since line k is perpendicular to line j, its slope must be $-\dfrac{2}{3}$. Thus, $y = \dfrac{2}{3}x + b$. Again, plug in (2,1) to get $y = -\dfrac{2}{3}x + \dfrac{7}{3}$.

4. **B** The equation $D = 600 + 0.05T$ is in the form $y = mx + b$, in which 600 is the b. Therefore, 600 is the y-intercept: it is the y-value for which $x = 0$. So, at time $= 0$, y is 600, and so 600 is the starting point, the depth at low tide.

5. **B** Great question; most SATs have one like this. Alex knew that $b = 4$, so the y intercept is 4, and that a is positive, so the graph rises from left to right. (Review slope in Skill 11 if needed. If you slacked during the slope chapter and did not do the drills, e-mail me and I'll send a motivational speech your way.) Choice B is the only choice that satisfies both requirements of y intercept of 4 and positive slope.

Skill 31 (page 73)

Arrangements

1. **6** Draw a blank for each option. Then write in the number of possibilities that can fill each option. There are two slogan options and three size options, so $2 \times 3 = 6$. Notice that this question is simple enough to do without the strategy, you could just picture shirts in piles, like at Old Navy, with two different slogans available in S, M, and L, making six piles.

2. **D** Draw a blank for each role that needs to be filled by an actor. Then write in the number of

actors who can fill the role. Remember that each actor can play only one role, so once someone is assigned, that actor can't be used again. Then multiply.

$\underline{5} \times \underline{4} \times \underline{3} \times \underline{2} \times \underline{1} = 120.$

3. **15** Draw a blank for each member of the doubles team. Write in the number of possible girls who can fill each slot; remember that once someone is assigned a position, she cannot also play another position. Then multiply. This question has one extra step since this is a team of two. It does not matter if it's Jenny and Jill or Jill and Jenny; we divide our answer by 2 since we will have double-counted each duo.

$\underline{6} \times \underline{5} = 30 \div 2 = 15$

4. **C** Draw a blank for each digit of the four-digit number. Fill in the number of possible digits that can go in each blank. No digit can be used more than once. So, $\underline{4} \times \underline{3} \times \underline{2} \times \underline{1} = 24.$

5. **64** Draw a blank for each digit of the three-digit number. Fill in the number of possible digits that can go in each blank. There are 4 prime numbers that can fill each blank: 2, 3, 5, and 7. Remember that 1 is not prime, but 2 is. Notice that the question does not say that a digit can be used only once. So, $\underline{4} \times \underline{4} \times \underline{4} = 64.$

6. **C** Draw a blank for each slot of the four-digit number. Write the number of possible digits that can fill each blank, filling choice in restricted slots first. The first digit has 9 possibilities, 1–9. It cannot be 0 since that would make the number a three-digit, not a four-digit, number. The next two slots can be 10 possibilities, 0–9. And the last digit can be 5 possibilities that would make the four-digit number even, 0, 2, 4, 6, 8. Then multiply.

$\underline{9} \times \underline{10} \times \underline{10} \times \underline{5} = 4,500.$

7. **48** Draw a blank for each of the five symbols that we will place. Fill in the restricted slots first; since the γ is never in the middle three spots, fill in these first. Once a symbol is placed, we can't use it again, so the middle slots have 4, 3, and 2 possibilities. Then either end slot can include the γ, so there are 2 and 1 possibilities. Fill in the slots and multiply.

$\underline{2} \times \underline{4} \times \underline{3} \times \underline{2} \times \underline{1} = 48.$

8. **C** Draw a blank for each position to be filled. Then fill in the restricted slots first; there are only three players able to pitch or catch. Once a pitcher is chosen, two are left to possibly catch. Once the pitcher and catcher are chosen, there are four kids still available for the remaining positions. Fill in these slots and multiply.

$\underline{3} \times \underline{2} \times \underline{4} \times \underline{3} \times \underline{2} = 144.$

Pitcher Catcher   Other   Other   Other

Skill 32 (page 75)

Long Word No-Problems

1. **A** Peter and Stacy will sell 90% of their crops, so:

corn   tomatoes

$(0.90)(5,000)(0.35) + (0.90)(10,000)(0.74) = \$8,235.$

2. **C** Simply translate. Evan pays a \$65 flat fee plus \$5 for every 3 movies. So his total cost is $65 + 5(492 \div 3) = \$885.$

3. **D** We can't use a calculator on this one, so we have to add the fractions. The common denominator is 15, so:

$$3\frac{4}{5} + 4\frac{2}{3}$$

$$3\frac{4(3)}{5(3)} + 4\frac{2(5)}{3(5)}$$

$$3\frac{12}{15} + 4\frac{10}{15}$$

$$7\frac{22}{15} - 8\frac{7}{15}$$

Since $8\frac{7}{15}$ is a bit less than 8.5, the answer is D.

4. **C** Translate: 3 cases with 12 two-pint containers means $(3)(12)(2) = 72$ pints. The same amount of berries would be in $72 \div 3 = 24$ three-pint containers.

5. **C** Most of the word problem just describes the equation. Once you realize that, you just plug the given numbers into the equation and solve for the unknown.

$A = P(1 + r)^{tn}$
$A = 500(1 + 0.05)^{(2)(3)}$
$A = 670.047$
Rounding to the nearest dollar, we get \$670.05.

Skill 33 (page 77)

What You Really Want . . . Probability

1. **B** Probability $= \dfrac{\text{want}}{\text{total}}$, so the probability of selecting a blue marble is $\dfrac{4}{12}$. This question requires that we reduce the $\dfrac{4}{12}$ to $\dfrac{1}{3}$. No problem, stop looking at me like that, reducing is easy, just divide the top and bottom of the fraction by the same number. Or, if you really don't like reducing, just use your calculator. Divide 4 by 12 to get 0.333. Then divide each answer choice (top by the bottom) to get decimals and see which one matches 0.333. Nice.

2. $\boxed{\dfrac{1}{3}} = 0.333$ Great vocab review! Remember that 1 is not a prime number. So since Probability $= \dfrac{\text{want}}{\text{total}}$, the probability of randomly selecting a prime number from the set is $\dfrac{2}{6} = \dfrac{1}{3} = 0.333$. When you take the SAT, remember that if you have a long decimal number, you have to use enough digits to fill in the student-produced response grid, so 0.33 would be marked wrong and we need 0.333!

3. **D** Since the probability of selecting a carrot is 1 out of 4, there are 4 vegetables in the basket or a multiple of 4 since $\dfrac{1}{4}$ could be a reduced version of the actual number. Thus, only choice D works since 8 is the only multiple of 4 in the choices.

4. **C** Since Probability $= \dfrac{\text{want}}{\text{total}}$ and the probability of obscenities is $\dfrac{7}{12}$, there are 7 scenes with obscenities for every 12 scenes of the movie. Thus, there are 5 scenes of nonobscenities, $12 - 7 = 5$. $n = 5$ and $c = 7$, so $= \dfrac{n}{c} = \dfrac{5}{7}$.

5. $\boxed{\dfrac{1}{4}}$ Since the question states that either team has an equal chance of winning, the probability

of Northampton winning each game is 1 out of 2, or $\dfrac{1}{4}$. The probability of winning both games is $\dfrac{1}{2} \times \dfrac{1}{2} = \dfrac{1}{4}$.

6. **B** Since Probability $= \dfrac{\text{want}}{\text{total}}$ and Toula won 10 out of the total of 21 games recorded in the table that were won in Northampton, $\dfrac{10}{21} = 0.476 = 47.6\%$.

For this type question that asks for a probability from data in a table, identify where the data mentioned in the question show up in the table, in this case, "games that were won in Northampton."

Skill 34 (page 79)

He's Making a List . . . Median, Mode, and Range

1. **28** Simply draw blanks for the seven numbers and place 31 in the middle blank. Then fill in the consecutive numbers above and below 31. "Consecutive" means numbers ordered from highest to lowest or lowest to highest for example, 28, 29, 30, 31, 32, 33, 34. So the smallest number is 28.

2. **25** Range is the spread of values, that is, the largest minus the smallest, so $150 - 125 = 25$.

3. **A** First add Don's score to the table—there are now two bowlers who scored a 140. The mode is the number in the list that occurs most often. According to the table there are four bowlers who scored 130, so 130 is the mode. Then to find the median, rewrite the data as a list in order. The middle number is 135, and the median minus the mode is $135 - 130 = 5$.

4. **A** Simply plug each answer in for the variable. If $m = 2$, then the list is 2, 5, 2 and $2m - 2$, which equals 2, is the mode.

5. **D** Increasing the largest number does not affect the median. No matter how big the biggest number becomes, the middle number is still in the middle of the list. If you were unsure for this question, you could simply make up a list of nine numbers and try the choices and see

which ones change the median and which one does not.

6. **453** Rewrite the attendance numbers from the table as a list in order. Since the question states that 452 should be the median, x must be to the right of 452. The question states that no numbers are the same. So any number greater than 452 will make 452 the median, and the least x can equal is 453. Notice how simple this "hard" question is if you know the vocab and how to approach it!

Skill 35 (page 82)

$y = ax^2 + bx + c$

1. **B** On the SAT, when you are given a point (x, y) and an equation, plug the point into the equation. So plug $(0, k)$ into either equation. $k = 2(0)^2 + 3(0) + 4 = 4$. So $k = 4$.

2. **B** Rewrite $y - 2 = -(x + 3)^2$ so it matches the form $y = (x - h)^2 + k$. Just add 2 to both sides to get $y = -(x + 3)^2 + 2$. In this form, the vertex, which is also known as the minimum/maximum point, is (h, k), so $(-3, 2)$ is the maximum point.

3. **B** Answer choice B is in intercept form of a quadratic equation and gives the correct intercepts of 3 and −2. Answer choices C and D are in vertex form, which gives the vertex of the parabola, not the x-intercepts.

4. **3** Plug in 0 for the y. Remember that if this were a function question, $f(x)$ also means y, so you'd plug in 0 for the $f(x)$. Anyway, we get:

   $0 = 5x^2 - 10x - 15$
   $0 = x^2 - 2x - 3$. Simplify by dividing both sides by 5.
   $0 = (x - 3)(x + 1)$ factor
   $x = 3$ or $x = -1$.

   The question asks for the positive value of x, so the correct answer is $x = 3$.

5. **2.84** We can't factor this equation as we did in question number 4 above, so to solve for x, we need to use the quadratic formula. You need to memorize this for the SAT. It comes up fairly often. The quadratic formula is

   $x = \dfrac{-b \pm \sqrt{b^2 - 4ac}}{2a}$. In the equation from the

question, $a = 5$, $b = -10$, and $c = -12$, so plug these into the formula, and we get:

$$x = \frac{-(-10) \pm \sqrt{(-10)^2 - 4(5)(-12)}}{2(5)}$$

$$x = \frac{10 \pm \sqrt{100 + 240}}{2(5)}$$

$$x = \frac{10 \pm \sqrt{340}}{10} = 2.84 \, .$$

Remember that you must grid 2.84; you won't get credit for 2.8.

6. **4** When the ball hits the ground, height is zero, so plug $h = 0$ into the equation and solve for t.

   $0 = -4.9t^2 + 20t$
   $0 = -t(4.9t - 20)$

   $t = 0$ and $\dfrac{20}{4.9} = 4$

7. **B** On the SAT, when you are given a point (x, y) and an equation, plug the point into the equation. So plug $(m, 4)$ into either equation. Since 0 is the only solution that works, there is one solution. CARELESS ERROR BUSTER: Notice that the correct answer is B (1 solution), not A (0); make sure to answer the final question asked, in this case not "what is the solution" but "how many" solutions.

8. **A** Plug $(m, 22)$ into the first equation to solve for m. Then plug the solution into the second equation to solve for k.

   $22 = 2(m)^2 + 4$
   $18 = 2(m)^2$
   $9 = m^2$
   $+3$ or $-3 = m$.

   Plug $(3, 22)$ or $(-3, 22)$ into the second equation.
   $22 = -(3)^2 - k$
   $22 = -9 - k$
   $31 = -k$
   $-31 = k$.

9. **D** This type of question is rated "hard," but is easy for us. Since k is negative, the U-shaped graph must open down; and since r is negative, the y intercept must be negative. Choice D is the only answer that satisfies both requirements.

Skill 36 (page 85)

Circles

1. **A** The question describes a circle. That's what a circle is, it's all the points in a plane that are a certain distance from a center point. Remember that the radius is the distance from the center to the circle, and the diameter is twice that distance, that is, twice the radius.

2. **C** The center is (h, k) based on the equation $(x - h)^2 + (y - k)^2 = r^2$. So match up the given equation to $(x - h)^2 + (y - k)^2 = r^2$ and determine h and k. For $(x - 8)^2 + (y + 2)^2 = 49$, $h = 8$ and $k = -2$. Notice that we have $(y + 2)$, but the formula is for $(y - k)$, so we switch the sign of 2 to get -2. So, the center is $(8, -2)$.

3. **D** We just need to apply the information we are given into the equation for a circle, which is $(x - h)^2 + (y - k)^2 = r^2$. Since the center is $(5, -3)$ and the radius is 6, $h = 5$, $k = -3$, and $r = 6$. So D is the answer. Notice that we can easily get this question with the process of elimination. For example, since $r = 6$, the number to the right of the equals sign, r^2, must equal 36, not 6.

4. **D** When a picture is described but not shown, draw it. The circle has center $(1, 4)$. Since it is tangent to the y-axis, our sketch shows that it has a radius of 1. So $h = 1$, $k = 4$, and $r = 1$. Choice D works.

5. **D** When a picture is described but not shown, draw it. The sketch shows that the center must be $(3, 3)$ and that the radius is therefore 3. So $h = 3$, $k = 3$, and $r = 3$. Choice D works. Watch out for choice B, which looks okay but has a minus sign instead of a plus sign between the parentheses! That's why you've got to cut out the flash cards at the end of this book and memorize the equation for a circle.

6. **5** The given equation is not in the standard form for a circle, $(x - h)^2 + (y - k)^2 = r^2$, so we need to complete the square to put it into standard form, as follows:

$$x^2 + 6x + y^2 - 4y = 12$$
$$(x^2 + 6x + 9) - 9 + (y^2 - 4y + 4) - 4 = 12$$
$$(x + 3)^2 + (y - 2)^2 - 13 = 12$$
$$(x + 3)^2 + (y - 2)^2 = 25.$$

Skill 37 (page 87)

Hopscotch, Pigtails, and Remainders

1. **B** Your calculator tells you that 13 divided by 3 is 4.3333. That does not give us the answer. Instead we need to channel 5th grade: you haven't showered in a week, and you're sure that this next pack of baseball cards will complete your set. Now you remember, remainder is just the left over when you do long division.

$$\begin{array}{r} 4r1 \\ 3\overline{)13} \\ \underline{12} \\ 1 \end{array}$$

2. **A** Just divide 24 by even numbers and see which answers we can cross off.

$$\begin{array}{r} 1r10 \\ 14\overline{)24} \\ \underline{14} \\ 10 \end{array} \quad \begin{array}{r} 1r8 \\ 16\overline{)24} \\ \underline{16} \\ 8 \end{array} \quad \begin{array}{r} 1r6 \\ 18\overline{)24} \\ \underline{18} \\ 6 \end{array} \quad \begin{array}{r} 1r4 \\ 20\overline{)24} \\ \underline{20} \\ 4 \end{array}$$

So the answer is 12, since all the other answer choices can be remainders when 24 is divided by even numbers.

3. **D** This is a great review of the "Use the Answers" strategy. Just try each answer choice to see which one does not give remainder 3 when divided by 4.

$$\begin{array}{r} 1r3 \\ 4\overline{)7} \\ \underline{4} \\ 3 \end{array} \quad \begin{array}{r} 3r3 \\ 4\overline{)15} \\ \underline{12} \\ 3 \end{array} \quad \begin{array}{r} 4r3 \\ 4\overline{)19} \\ \underline{16} \\ 3 \end{array} \quad \begin{array}{r} 5r2 \\ 4\overline{)22} \\ \underline{20} \\ 2 \end{array}$$

Each choice works EXCEPT choice D, 22, which gives a remainder of 2 not 3.

4. **A** This is a nice vocab review. Remember that "consecutive" means in a row, "positive" means greater than 0, and "integer" means no decimals. So just choose five consecutive positive integers and divide each by 4, and see which answer choice is correct. Remember that the correct answer might be a different starting point, but the same pattern as your numbers.

5. **D** This is a great preview of "Weird Symbol Questions" (Skill 45). This is not some symbol that you missed in algebra class. Nobody knows this symbol. The SAT is making it up

and telling us what to do with it. So you just have to stay confident and roll with it. The symbol represents the remainder when the second number is divided by the first. So n divided by −18 should give a remainder of 3. Simply try each answer choice. 39 divided by −18 equals −2 with a remainder of 3.

6. **C** Another preview of "Weird Symbol Questions." The operation just represents the remainder when the first number is divided by the second number. So 24 divided by b should give a remainder of 3. What can b equal to make that work? Here's the key: if the remainder is 3, then we must multiply to get 24 − 3 = 21. So we can divide by 7 or 21 to get a remainder of 3, and there are two possibilities. This is a "hard" because most people who do not read this book have absolutely no idea how to do this question.

Skill 38 (page 89)

Absolute Value

1. **C** Great "Use the Answers" review! Try each answer choice in the equation. Choice C is correct, since $|6 - 18| = |-12| = 12$ and $|6 - (-6)| = |12| = 12$.

2. **D** Again, "Use the Answers." Try each answer choice in the question.

   I. $|2 + 3| = 5$ correct

   II. $|-2 + 3| \neq 5$ incorrect

   III. $|-8 + 3| = 5$ correct

   So I and III are correct, and choice D is the answer.

3. **D** Remember to underline the vocab term "negative integers" so you don't forget about it. We must consider the possible values for m and n:

   $|-7| + |-1| = 8, m = -7, n = -1$
   $|-6| + |-2| = 8, m = -6, n = -2$
   $|-5| + |-3| = 8, m = -5, n = -3$
   $|-4| + |-4| = 8, m = -4, n = -4$
   $|-3| + |-5| = 8, m = -3, n = -5$
   $|-2| + |-6| = 8, m = -2, n = -6$
   $|-1| + |-7| = 8, m = -1, n = -7$

So try each possible pair of m and n to see which gives the least value for $m - n$.

$-7 - (-1) = -6$ and is the least value.

4. **D** Since $x < 0$, x must equal −12 since $|4 + (-12)| = |-8| = 8$. And in the equation $|3 - y| = 5$, y equals −2 since $|3 - (-2)| = 5$. So $xy = (-12)(-2) = 24$.

5. $\boxed{-1 < a < 0}$ Start by just trying some numbers and see if you can get one that works. Any positive numbers yield an answer that is too large, and 0 is still too big since $|1 + 2(0)| = 1$. So try −1. $|1 + 2(-1)| = |-1| = 1$, so that doesn't work. What if $a = -0.52$. That works, so −0.5 is an answer; in fact any number between 0 and −1 works.

6. **D** Let's look at each choice. Could m equal
   I. 0   Definitely, $0 = |0|$.
   II. n Sure, $n = |n|$ could work if $n > 0$.
   III. $-n$ Sure, $-n = |n|$, if $n < 0$. Nice!
   So all three work.

7. **A** child with a height between 48 and 68 inches can ride. 58 is the middle of that range and a child can ride if he or she is within 10 inches of that midpoint. Therefore, answer choice B is correct. Choice B represents all numbers that are within 10 of 58, that is, the range 48 to 68. Note: You can also simply Make It Real and try a few heights that should or should not work and see which answer choice works. For example, try a height of 68 inches, which should satisfy the equation, and a height of 70, which should not. Answer choice A is the only one that passes both tests.

Skill 39 (page 91)

Sequences

Answer to Brian's Math Magic Trick #2: Come on, you should know that there are no elephants in Denmark! To find out how this stunning act of magic works, go to my website: www.BrianLeaf.com/Elephants.

1. **B** Subtract 47 − 14 = 33 and divide that number by 3 since we need to add some number three times to get from 14 to 47. Now 33/3 = 11, so 11 is the number we add each time. Don't be fooled by choice A; 11 is not the answer—it is the number we add to get the answer. 14 + 11 =

25, and 25 + 11 = 36, and 36 + 11 = 47. So 25 and 36 are the numbers that fill the two blanks. You could also just "Use the Answers" to get this question; just try the choices and see which one works. "Use the Answers" is one heck of a strategy!

2. **A** Draw this out: _, –5, 12. Since it's an "arithmetic" sequence, we know that we add some number each time to get the next term. So, –5 + x = 12. Add 5 to both sides and x = 17. So we add 17 to each term to get the next one. Therefore, the missing first term is x + 17 = –5. Don't let this be daunting; just subtract 17 from each side to get –22. You could also do this in your head rather than set up the algebra, or you could, of course, "Use the Answers" and just try the choices to see which one works.

3. **B** A geometric sequence is just a super-fancy term for a list of numbers where you multiply each member by the same number to arrive at the next member on the list. To find that number, just notice what it is, or divide a term by the one before it. –2/4 = –0.5. So –0.5 is the number you multiply each term by. The next term is $-\dfrac{1}{2} \times -0.5 = +0.25$, which matches choice B, $0.25 = \dfrac{1}{4}$.

4. **A** There are several ways to answer this question. The best way is to whip out your calculator and give it an Air Jordan—just do it. Just add up the 20 terms: 12 + 15 + 18 + 21 + 24 + 27 + 30 + ... This is much easier than people think. It's totally the way to go. I just timed myself doing this method, and adding up the 20 terms took only 36 seconds. You can even take your time to avoid a careless error. And even if your answer is a little off, you'll probably be able to choose the right answer choice. Notice how far apart they are, so even a close estimate will get you the right one. Not too bad for an easy and flawless way to get a "hard" question right! The other two ways are to write out a bunch of the numbers until you see a pattern that you can use to predict the sum or to memorize the silly arithmetic sequence sum formula: sum = (0.5)(number terms)[2(first term) + (number terms – 1) (difference between terms)]. So sum = s = (0.5)(20)[2(12) + 19(3)] = 810.

Skill 40 (page 93)

Not So Complex Numbers

1. **C** "Product" means multiply, so –2i(3i + 2) = –6i^2 – 4i. Replace i^2 with (–1) to get –6(–1) – 4i, which equals 6 – 4i. CARELESS ERROR BUSTER: Remember to distribute the negative.

2. **C** Great FOIL review. The square of (i – 2) means (i – 2)(i – 2). So just FOIL (i – 2)(i – 2) to get i^2 – 2i – 2i + 4 and collect like terms to get i^2 – 4i + 4. Normal FOILing and you'd be done, but here there is one last step, the key to complex number questions. Since i^2 actually equals –1, we substitute –1 in for i^2 to get –1 – 4i + 4, and we collect like terms to get a final answer of 3 – 4i.

3. **C** To simplify an expression with an i in the denominator (bottom) of a fraction, multiply by the conjugate as follows:

$$\dfrac{6i}{2 - i} =$$

$$\dfrac{6i(2 + i)}{(2 - i)(2 + i)} = \quad \text{multiply top and bottom of fraction by the } (2 + i)\text{, the conjugate of } (2 - i)$$

$$\dfrac{12i + 6i^2}{4 + 2i - 2i - i^2} =$$

$$\dfrac{12i + (6)(-1)}{4 - (-1)} = \quad \text{replace } i \text{ squared with –1 and simplify}$$

$$\dfrac{12i - 6}{5}.$$

4. **D** Since i^2 = –1, and since i^4 means (i^2)(i^2), we know that i^4 = (–1)(–1) = 1.

5. **D** Don't be intimidated. Just multiply tops and bottoms as in normal fraction multiplication. Remember that the bottoms of (1 – i) and (1 + i) get FOILed:

$$\dfrac{1}{1 - i} \cdot \dfrac{1 - i}{1 + i} = \dfrac{1 - i}{1 + i - i - i^2} = \dfrac{1 - i}{1 - i^2} = \dfrac{1 - i}{1 - (-1)} = \dfrac{1 - i}{2}$$

6. **D** Ditto question 5, "Don't be intimidated." This is a great review of factoring. You can multiply tops and bottoms just like normal fraction multiplication, or even better you can remember to cross-cancel first. How do you

know to do that? "Springboard," baby! Whenever you see $x^2 - y^2$, factor it, even if it is disguised as $1 - i^2$. Remember that $x^2 - y^2$ is the SAT's favorite kind of factoring, so watch for it. Once you notice it, it's easy to see what to do next. Don't you love our Mantras! So

$$\frac{5i}{1-i} \cdot \frac{1-i^2}{1+i} = \frac{5i}{1-i} \cdot \frac{(1-i)(1+i)}{1+i} = 5i \text{ , since the}$$

$(1-i)(1+i)$ on the tops and bottoms cancel out.

Skill 41 (page 95)

Don't Even Think About It! . . . Most Common SAT Math Careless Errors I

1. **B** Nice function review! $f(-p)$ means plug $-p$ in for x. So $f(-p) = -2(-p)^3 = -2(-p^3) = 2p^3$. CARELESS ERROR BUSTER: Remember that the 2 is not inside the parentheses and does not get cubed with the p.

2. **A** Plug in $m = -1$ and simplify. $m(2x^2 - 2) = -1(2x^2 - 2) = -2x^2 + 2$. CARELESS ERROR BUSTER: Remember to distribute the negative sign!

3. **D** Plug $x = 3$ into the equation to get

   $y = \frac{3(a) - 15}{3} = a - 5$, not $a - 15$. CARELESS

   ERROR BUSTER: Remember to also divide the

   15 by 3.

4. **C** Plug $2p$ in for m and then FOIL $(2p + 4)^2$. You can use the algebra trick for FOILing a binomial if you know it, and if you don't, no sweat, just do it out: $(2p + 4)^2 = (2p + 4)(2p + 4) = 4p^2 + 8p + 8p + 16 = 4p^2 + 16p + 16$. Skill 42 Preview: When you FOIL, remember the middle term!

5. **A** Another function review, this is a good day. This question is similar to number 3 above, but more involved. Plug $-2p$ in for x: $f(-2p) = -2p(2(-2p)^2 - 2) = -2p(2(4p^2) - 2) = -2p(8p^2 - 2) = -16p^3 + 4p$. CARELESS ERROR BUSTER: Remember to distribute the negative sign!

6. **360** Serious functions review! In the $g(x)$ function, plug m in for x and 27 in for the result: $27 = 3m$, so $m = 9$. Next, plug $-2m$, which we now know equals -18, into the f function: $-18(-18 - 2) = -18(-20) = +360$. Skill 42 Preview: Finish the

question, don't stop with $m = 9$. Remember to ask, "Did I finish the question?"

7. **16** Plug 5 into the g function and plug 1 into the f function and then subtract as follows:
   $g(5) - f(1)$
   $3x - x(x - 2)$
   $3(5) - \{1(1 - 2)\}$
   $15 - (1 - 2)$
   $15 - (-1) = 16$.
   CARELESS ERROR BUSTER: Watch the negative sign!

Skill 42 (page 97)

Don't Even Think About It! . . . Most Common SAT Math Careless Errors II

1. **C** Nice function review! $f(4p)$ means plug $4p$ in for x. So $f(4p) = 3(4p)^2 = 3(16p^2) = 48p^2$. CARELESS ERROR BUSTER: Remember that the 4 gets squared and that only then do you multiply by 3, not before—order of operations, my man.

2. **14** When $x = -2$, then $y = 2(-2)^2 + 4 = 12$. The question does not ask for y, but for $y + 2$, so the correct answer is $12 + 2 = 14$. This is weird since your math teacher always asks for a final answer of y, not $y + 2$. But we know the SAT does this, and we know to watch for it. CARELESS ERROR BUSTER: Remember to finish the question.

3. **B** If he rode 5 miles in 10 minutes, we could say he rode 1 mile per 2 minutes. When he later rode to his friend's house 4 miles away, it would take him (4 miles)(2 minutes/mile) = 8 minutes. CARELESS ERROR BUSTER: Remember to finish the question. 1 and 2 are offered as choices, don't finish the first calculation and go, "Sweet, there it is." Remember to finish. Ask yourself, "Did I finish the question?"

4. **D** Plug $3y$ for x into the expression $(x - 2)^2$ to get $(3y - 2)^2 = 9y^2 - 12y + 4$. CARELESS ERROR BUSTER: When you FOIL a binomial, remember the middle term.

5. **16** Plug -6 in for x: $r(-6) = \frac{-6}{3} = -2 = n$.

Some people would stop here, but remember to finish the question. To find $p(-2n)$, plug -2 in for n, so $p(-2n) = p(-2(-2)) = p(4) = 2(4)(4-2) = 16$. CARELESS ERROR BUSTER: Remember to finish the question.

6. **3** Most kids have a tough time with this one. The key is that the distance is equal for both trips, so we set (rate)(time) equal for the way there and the way back:

(Rate)(time) = (rate)(time).

The total trip was 0.5 hour. So if we call one way t, then we can call the return trip $(0.5 - t)$.

Notice that we should use hours, not minutes, since rate is in miles per hour.

$10(t) = (15)(0.5 - t)$

$10t = 7.5 - 15t$

$25t = 7.5$

$t = 0.3$ hour.

Now remember, the question asks how far Josh lives, NOT the time, so $D = RT$ and $D = 10$ mph(0.3 hour) = 3 miles. CARELESS ERROR BUSTER: Finish the question, don't stop with $t = 0.3$. Remember to ask, "Did I finish the question?"

Skill 43 (page 99)

Misbehaving Numbers: Weird Number Behavior

1. **0** Since $k = 0$, q must equal zero, since $2kp = 2(0)p = 0$. Anything times zero equals zero.

2. **D** Point N is to the left of -4, so it must be more negative than -4. Choice D is the only choice that is more negative than -4.

3. **C** To multiply to get zero, either $(x - 2) = 0$ or $(x + 3) = 0$. So $x = 2$ or -3.

4. **C** Great review of "Make It Real." Plug $m = -2$ and a value for n, say $n = 3$, into each answer choice and look for the greatest result. Choice C is correct because the even exponent cancels out the negative sign, whereas the odd exponent in choice D keeps the negative.

5. **B** Great "Use the Answers" review. Try each answer in the question:

   Ⓐ Nope, $-1 \neq 2(-1)$
   Ⓑ Yup, $0 = 2(0)$
   Ⓒ Nope, $1 \neq 2(1)$
   Ⓓ Nope, $2 \neq 2(2)$

Choice B is the answer since anything times zero equals zero.

6. **C** "Make It Real!" Let's say $r = -2$. Plug $r = -2$ into each choice and find the greatest one.

   Choice C is greatest since subtracting a negative is like adding: $2 - (-2) = 4$.

7. **C** "Make It Real!" Let's say $x = -1.5$. Then $x = -1.5$, $x^2 = (-1.5)^2 = +2.25$, and $x^3 = (-1.5)^3 = -3.375$. So the order is $x^3 < x < x^2$, since when you square a negative, it becomes positive, but when you cube a negative, it stays negative.

Skill 44 (page 101)

Mathematical Transformations

1. **B** The graph shown is a transformation of the parent $y = x^2$ moved down 1 unit, so $y = x^2 - 1$. You could also "Use the Answers" and graph each answer choice on your calculator to see which one matches the graph shown in the question.

2. **C** This is a straightforward transformation. The parent function $g(x)$ needs to be shifted 1 unit to the right. If you memorize the transformations listed in this Skill, the question is easy; a right transformation would be $y = g(x - 1)$. If you did not memorize the transformations, get to it, you silly slacker. Or, you could graph each choice on your calculator and see which one yields results that are all 1 unit to the right of the parent.

3. **D** This is a transformation. The graph shown in the question is $y = x^2$ moved 1 unit left. To also move it down 2 units would result in the equation $y = (x + 1)^2 - 2$. You could "Use the Answers" and use your calculator to graph each answer choice to see which one shows the graph from the question moved 2 units down.

4. **D** You can see that n is a transformation of m, and using a pair of points as reference, you can see that it has been moved up 1 unit and left 2 units. So, based on the equation $n(x) = m(x + h) - k$, $h = 2$ and $k = -1$. So $h - k = 2 - (-1) = 3$.

Skill 45 (page 103)

SohCahToa!

1. **B** We always want to mark all the info from the question into the diagram. And sometimes

the SAT does that for us. Here all information is marked. Thanks, SAT. So don't get caught up in the complex wording of the question. Look at the diagram. It's a straightforward SohCahToa question. The key to SohCahToa questions is simply to determine which ratio we need for the question. All we have to do is look at the information given. If we are given opposite and hypotenuse, we use sin. If we are given adjacent and hypotenuse, we use cos. And if we are given opposite and adjacent, we use tan. That's it. So based on the 40° angle, we have the adjacent leg and want the opposite leg. So, we use tan:

$$\tan = \frac{\text{opposite}}{\text{adjacent}}$$

$$\tan 40 = \frac{x}{4}$$

$0.839 = \frac{x}{4}$ use your calculator to get the value of tan 40, which is 0.839

$3.36 = x$. multiply both sides by 4

2. **B** Remember that sin, cos, and tan are talking about right triangles, so draw a diagram. Sin

represents $\frac{\text{opposite}}{\text{hypotenuse}}$, so since $\sin A = \frac{3}{5}$, we

know that the opposite leg of vertex A equals 3 and the hypotenuse equals 5. Whenever you have two sides of a right triangle, use $a^2 + b^2 = c^2$ to get the third side. Great mighty Pythagoras review (Skill 24). So $3^2 + b^2 = 5^2$ and $b = 4$.

Therefore, $\tan A = \frac{\text{opposite}}{\text{adjacent}} = \frac{3}{4}$, since the

opposite leg equals 3, and the adjacent leg equals 4.

3. **A** $\sin B = \frac{\text{opposite}}{\text{hypotenuse}}$. In the diagram, the leg

opposite vertex B equals 5, and the hypotenuse

equals 7. So $\sin B = \frac{\text{opposite}}{\text{hypotenuse}} = \frac{5}{7}$.

4. **D** $\cos Z = \frac{\text{adjacent}}{\text{hypotenuse}}$. In the diagram, the leg

adjacent to vertex Z equals 4, and the hypotenuse

equals 5. So $\cos Z = \frac{\text{adjacent}}{\text{hypotenuse}} = \frac{4}{5} = 0.8$.

5. **B** sin and cos are equal when they are complementary. Memorize that; it shows up quite a bit

on the test. Actually, don't just memorize it; understand it. Think about it—in a right triangle *ABC*, the two non–right angles are always complementary and sin *A* and cos *B* are equal, so $\frac{\pi}{2}$ is the answer since $\frac{\pi}{2}$ equals 90°.

Skill 46 (page 105)

Beyond SohCahToa

1. **C** Awesome "Use the Answers" question! Try each answer choice, and use the process of elimination until you find the one choice that has values that all work. Choice C is correct since both 45 and 225 yield 1 when plugged in for θ in the expression tan θ. If you've studied trig, you could also do this question the "math class way." Since tan means "opposite over adjacent," tan θ = 1 when opposite = adjacent, and therefore sin θ = cos θ. So what are the values for θ where sin θ = cos θ? Sin could equal cos when θ is between 0 and 90 or between 180 and 270, because in these regions sin and cos are either both positive or both negative. Use the process of elimination, and only choice C has answers in these two regions.

2. **A** Follow the directions given for the law of sines. The ratio of a side and the sin of its opposite angle is equal for all sides. So

$\frac{32}{\sin 74} = \frac{27}{\sin 54} = \frac{x}{\sin 52}$. Perimeter equals the

sum of the sides of the triangle, and we already know two of the sides. We can use that ratio to

solve for *x*, the third side. So since $\frac{32}{\sin 74} = \frac{x}{\sin 52}$,

we can cross-multiply to get $(x)(\sin 74) = (32)$ $(\sin 52)$ and divide both sides by sin 74 to get

$\frac{32 \sin 52}{\sin 74} = x$. Therefore, the perimeter equals

$59 + \frac{32 \sin 52}{\sin 74}$.

3. **C** Secant and cosecant would be complementary if $K = 90°$ or $\frac{\pi}{2}$ radians.

4. **C** In the equation $y = a \sin b(x - c) - d$, the *c* tells how far left or right the graph was moved from the origin, and *d* tells how far up or down the graph was moved from the origin. So this graph will always reach a minimum of −1 −*d*,

157

since its normal minimum is −1 and it has been shifted down d units, giving a new minimum of $-1 -d$.

Skill 47 (page 108)

Directly and Inversely Proportional

1. **B** For "y to be directly proportional to x," each y must equal a constant (a number) multiplied by each x. Choice B is correct since each x multiplied by 5 yields each y.

2. **5** "y is directly proportional to x^2" means $\dfrac{y}{x^2}$ $= a$. So we set up a proportion between the two sets of (x, y) values, cross-multiply, and solve for the unknown x. Remember Skill 20: when you see a proportion, cross-multiply.

   $\dfrac{y}{x^2} = \dfrac{y}{x^2} \Rightarrow \dfrac{18}{3^2} = \dfrac{50}{x^2}$ cross-multiply

   $18x^2 = (9)(50)$
   $18x^2 = 450$ divide both sides by 18
   $x^2 = 25$ take square root of both
   $x = 5$ sides

3. **D** Each y in the table is found by multiplying each x value by 5. So simply multiply $7.5 \times 5 = 37.5$.

4. **C** "y is inversely proportional to x" implies that $y = \dfrac{k}{x}$, and therefore $yx = k$. In other words, x times y should equal the same constant for each (x, y) pair in the table. Choice C is correct since x times y for each pair of values equals 108.

5. **D** Just choose an (x, y) pair from the table and try it in each answer choice. The one that works is the right answer. If two work, just try another (x, y) pair as a tie breaker.

6. **A** "y is inversely proportional to x^2" means $y = \dfrac{k}{x^2}$. Plug the first pair of values into this equation to find the value of k. $16 = \dfrac{k}{2^2}$. So $k = 64$.

   Now, using $k = 64$, plug the second pair of values $(x, \frac{1}{2})$ into the equation. $\dfrac{1}{2} = \dfrac{64}{x^2}$. Cross-multiply $x^2 = 128$, so $x = \sqrt{128} = \sqrt{64 \times 2} = 8\sqrt{2}$, or 11.3.

7. **C** "y varies inversely with x" means $y = \dfrac{k}{x}$. Plug the first pair of values into this equation to find the value of k. $10 = \dfrac{k}{3}$. So $k = 30$. Now, using $k = 30$, plug the second pair of values $(x, 8)$ into the equation. $8 = \dfrac{30}{x}$. Cross-multiply $8x = 30$, so $x = 3.75$.

Skill 48 (page 111)

Rational Expressions

1. **C** The common denominator is $(x - 3)(x + 3)$, so:

   $\dfrac{(3x + 9)(x + 3)}{(x - 3)(x + 3)} + \dfrac{(x + 2)(x - 3)}{(x + 3)(x - 3)} =$

   $\dfrac{3x^2 + 18x + 27}{(x - 3)(x + 3)} + \dfrac{x^2 - x - 6}{(x + 3)(x - 3)} =$

   $\dfrac{3x^2 + 18x + 27 + x^2 - x - 6}{(x - 3)(x + 3)} =$

   $\dfrac{4x^2 + 17x + 21}{(x - 3)(x + 3)}.$

2. **B** Recall from Skill 8 that a function is undefined if there is a negative inside a square root or if there is division by 0 (i.e., a zero in the bottom of a fraction), so in this case, if $x = 5$ or $x = -5$, we have division by zero, and the function would be undefined.

3. **−9 or 1** To clear out the fractions from this equation, multiply both sides by $(2)(x - 3)(x + 3)$ to get $-2(2)(x + 3) = 2(2)(x - 3) + (x - 3)(x + 3)$. Simplify this to get $-4x - 12 = 4x - 12 + x^2 - 9$. Collect like terms to get $x^2 + 8x - 9 = 0 = (x + 9)(x - 1)$, so $x = -9$ or 1.

Skill 49 (page 114)

How to Think Like a Math Genius I

1. **D** Proportions (Skill 20). When you see a proportion, cross-multiply. $3a = 60$, so $a = 20$.

2. **A** Average (Skill 3). The question asks for the sum, so use the sum formula: sum = (average) × (number of items). So sum = (14)(2) = 28.

3. Ⓒ Isosceles triangle (Skill 6) and triangle has 180° (Skill 4). If two sides of a triangle are equal, then two angles must also be equal, and since it is a triangle, the measures must add up to 180.

4. **150** Average (Skill 3). Since the average weight of the 5 boys is 120, their sum is $(120)(5) = 600$. When the sixth boy joins them, their weight cannot exceed 750 lb, so the sixth boy can weigh up to $750 - 600 = 150$.

5. Ⓒ Functions (Skill 15). $f(b) = 24$ means plug in b for x and 24 as the solution:
$24 = 3(b)^3$ divide by 3
$8 = b^3$ take cube root of both sides
$2 = b$.

6. **27** Ratios (Skill 19) and proportion (Skill 20). With the ratio of $2 : 3 : 4$, there are 9 total pieces of fruit. So set up a proportion for pear to total:
$\frac{3}{9} = \frac{9}{x}$ and cross-multiply to solve for x.
$81 = 3x$, so $x = 27$.

7. Ⓓ Functions (Skill 14). Plug 9 in for $M(u)$ and 6 (since June is the 6th month) in for u, and solve for k.
$9 = ((2)(6))^2 - k$
$9 = 144 - k$
$-135 = -k$
$135 = k$.

8. Ⓒ Make It Real (Skill 16). "Make It Real" turns this "hard" into an "easy." Choose numbers for the variables. Let's say $a = 9$ and $b = 8$. Then
I works since $ab = (9)(8) = 72$ which is a multiple of 12.
II flunks since $3a + 4b = (3)(9) + 4(8) = 59$ which is not a multiple of 12.
III works since $4a + 3b = (4)(9) + (3)(8) = 60$ which is a multiple of 12.
Since this is a late "medium," it's a good idea to test a second set of numbers to confirm that choices I and III both still work.

9. Ⓓ Geometry (Skill 4) and "What is a in terms of b and c?" (Skill 2). The best way to solve this question is to realize that the angles marked with a, b's, and c's add up to 360, since they are the four angles of a four-sided shape. Then it's easy since $a + 4b + 2c = 360$, and we just solve for a.

10. Ⓑ Averages (Skill 3). Set up the sum formula for each team. The sum of the first team is $170m$, and the sum for the second team is $182m$. Now, set up the average formula to determine the average of the groups combined: add the two sums $(170m + 182n)$ and divide by total bowlers $(m + n)$ and set equal to the combined average of 177.5. $\frac{170 + 182n}{m + n} = 177.5$. Algebraically manipulate to get m/n. OK, I admit it, this question is tough. Without our strategies very few students can get it. But our strategies knock it down from nearly impossible to possible.

Skill 50 (page 118)

How to Think Like a Math Genius II

1. Ⓐ Misbehaving Numbers (Skill 43), and Make It Real (Skill 16). Negative numbers with larger digits are smaller. Let's say $m = -3$. Then choice B equals $3m = 3(-3) = -9$. And -3 is actually larger than -9.

2. Ⓒ Misbehaving Numbers (Skill 43), and Make It Real (Skill 16). Let's say $p = -3$. $1 - p$ is largest since $1 - p = 1 - (-3) = 4$, while all other answers are negative.

3. Ⓐ Avoid Careless Errors (Skill 41) and Functions (Skill 14). Plug n in for x: $m(n) = 2(3n)^2 = 2(9n^2) = 18n^2$. Remember to square the 3 as well as the n, and then multiply by 2.

4. Ⓒ Logic (Skill 36). There are 42 yogis and 25 dungeon crawlers, so it would seem there are 67 total, but 18 are in both clubs, and have been counted twice. So at the joint meeting there are really $42 + 25 - 18 = 49$.

5. Ⓒ Translation (Skill 26), and Finish the Question (Skill 42). Translate the words into math and solve:
$0.5x - 4 = 0.3x$ add 4 to both sides
$0.5x = 0.3x + 4$ subtract $0.3x$
$0.2x = 4$ divide by 0.2
$x = 20$ remember to finish the question
$3x = 60$

6. Ⓓ Median and Mode (Skill 34), and Use the Answers (Skill 1). When you see a median or mode question, rewrite the data as a list

in order. Then try each answer choice. Choice D cannot be the value for p because it will make 7 tied with 3 as the mode.

7. **B** Logic (Skill 36) or Make It Real (Skill 16). B. There seem to be $m + p$ total members of sets M and P combined. Usually, we then subtract the common members (r) to determine the total, but in the "hard" question we subtract $2r$ since set Z contains **no** members that are in both. We are not just avoiding double-counting, but eliminating the common members entirely. So, set Z has $m + p - 2r$ members.

8. **10** Arrangements (Skills 31 & 32). Since we have one-on-one competition, we have two spots to fill, so draw two blanks. Five competitors can fill the first slot, and four can fill the second slot. Then multiply $5 \times 4 = 20$. Because, for example, Juan playing Ezra is the same as Ezra playing Juan, we divide by 2 and get $20/2 = 10$.

9. **C** Probability (Skill 33), Donut Area (Skill 18), or Use the Diagram (Skill 21).

Probability $= \dfrac{\text{want}}{\text{total}}$, so the probability of hitting the shaded region is
$$\frac{\text{Want}}{\text{Total}} = \frac{\text{shaded area}}{\text{total area}} = \frac{5^2\pi - 3.5\pi}{5^2\pi} = 0.51.$$
You could also just "Use the Diagram" and realize that no other answers make sense and that the shaded region being half the area of the larger circle is the only feasible answer.

10. **A** Absolute Value (Skill 38) and Misbehaving Numbers (Skill 43). When you see an absolute value question, remember to consider not only the obvious answer, but also the less obvious one. x can equal 7 or –1, and y can equal 1 or –5. So the greatest possible value for $x - y = 7 - (-5) = 12$.

Posttest I (page 125)

1. **B** This question looks impossible to some, but "Use the Answers" makes it easy! Try each choice. If $x = 1$, then $8^{1+1} = 2^{1+7}$ or $64 = 256$ which is not true. If $x = 2$, then $8^{2+1} = 2^{2+2}$ or $512 = 512$, so $x = 2$ is correct. Just to be sure, if there is time, you can try each of the other choices to

prove that no other choice works and that choice B is correct.

2. **B** "What is m in terms of p?" means solve for m, get m alone. Since $2m = 5n = 6p$, we can say that $2m = 6p$. Divide both sides by 2 and $m = 3p$.

3. **C** The sum of his grades is $10 \times 82 = 820$. The correct sum should have been 14 points higher (for the 5 and 9 points he was cheated on the 2 test grades). So the correct average is $834/10 = 83.4$, rounded to 83.

4. **142** The angles of any four-sided closed shape add up to 360, so the 4th angle equals $360 - 129 - 48 - 145 = 38$, and x forms a linear pair with 38, so $x = 180 - 38 = 142$.

5. **D** In two parallel lines, all big angles are equal and all small angles are equal. Since $x = 53$, it is a small angle. Redraw the diagram to reflect this. Then y is clearly a large angle and must equal $180 - 53 = 127$.

6. **B** As soon as you know that two sides in a triangle are equal, you know that the two angles opposite the two sides are also equal. Therefore, $a = c$. If $b = 160$, then $a + c + 160 = 180$, and $a + c = 20$. Since a equals c, a is half of 20, which is 10.

7. **30** Since $2x$ is the exterior angle of the triangle shown, $2x = x + 30$. Subtract x from both sides to get $x = 30$.

8. **12** Know your vocab terms and try numbers; the numbers can't be too big if they add up to 42. Or, you can divide 42 by 3 to get the middle number, and work from there. $12 + 14 + 16 = 42$.

9. **18** Know your vocab terms and try numbers. The number 36 is the lowest number that is a multiple of 4, 12, and 18.

10. **C** Add the two equations together so the y terms cancel, leaving $4x = 20$ and therefore $x = 5$. Plug $x = 5$ back into the equation and solve for y.

11. **C** Plug the two points into the slope equation:
$$\frac{3-0}{2-(-1)} = \frac{3}{3} = 1.$$

12. **C** Parallel lines have equal slopes, so the slope of the line is 3, and slope $\dfrac{3-p}{-1-(-2)} = 3$. "Use the Answers" or cross-multiply to solve for p. $p = 0$.

13. **D** The legend tells us that each ♥ represents 20 votes. Therefore, Scary received 90 votes and Posh Spice received 60, and $90 - 60 = 30$. Notice that half a heart equals half of 20, not half of 1.

14. **B** $f(-1) = -3(-1)^2 - 2 = -3 - 2 = -5$.

15. **B** This is a very common question on the SAT, showing up very often on recent tests. To solve, simply choose a pair of values such as (2, 6) and plug them into the answer choices for x and $f(x)$ to see in which choice the values work. Remember that $f(x)$ simply means y, so the table of values is a typical (x, y) table. To be sure of your answer, test the pair in all choices. If two answer choices work, choose a second (x, y) pair to determine which one is correct.

16. **C** This question seems theoretical and intimidating to some, but not to us with "Make It Real." Choose a real number in for t (remember, the question says that it must be negative). Let's say $t = -3$. Then try -3 for t in each answer choice to see which one does what the question asks, which one yields a positive number. If you get two or more answers that work, choose another real number for t until you get only one answer choice that works. Choice C is the answer since $3 - (-3) = 6$; in fact, subtracting a negative will always make it positive and that's why this is always the correct answer.

17. **D** Since the radius of circle B is half the diameter of circle A, it must be 8. Therefore, the area of circle B is Area $= \pi r^2 = \pi 8^2 = 64\pi$. You can also just check the scale on the figure, and, if needed, redraw the picture to scale to estimate which answer is correct.

18. **C** Perimeter is the addition of the sides. Since the perimeter of square $BCDF$ is 24, each side is 6. $AB = 12$ and $DE = 4$. Perimeter of the shaded region $= 18 + 4 + 6 + 6 + 12 + 10 = 56$.

19. **D** Remember that 1.4 to 2 is the same as saying "1.4 divided by 2," so just divide 1.4/2 on your calculator to get 0.7. Then divide each answer choice to see which one also gives 0.7. Easy!

20. **B** Set up the proportion and cross-multiply. $\dfrac{3}{35} = \dfrac{3.5}{x}$, so $3x = 122.5$. Divide by 3 to get $x = 40.83$ or $40\dfrac{5}{6}$. If the fractions in the answer choices scare you, just convert them to decimals.

21. **C** Draw point M into the diagram and estimate MD. Using geometry, this is a "hard" question because there are two steps using the Pythagorean theorem. But with "Use the Diagram," it's easy! If AB is 20, BC is 8, and DC is 4, then MD looks like somewhere between 10 and 15, probably in the middle. Translate the answer choices to decimals, and Choice C is correct.

22. **B** Easy, if you draw a diagram! The diagram shows that the sides of $ABCD$ are 6, 6, 3, and 7ish. So only answer choice B works. You could also use the Pythagorean theorem to get the exact length of side CB.

23. **B** Use the Pythagorean theorem.
$30^2 + p^2 = 34^2$
$900 + p^2 = 1156$
$p^2 = 256$
$p = 16$.

24. **B** Draw a diagram. When you see a right triangle, try $a^2 + b^2 = c^2$. You can also use special right triangles if you notice that 3 is half of 6.

25. **D** Triangles NBA and NMO are isosceles so base angles are equal. The triangles are similar since they also share a vertex angle ($\angle N$).

26. **115** Translate the words to math and solve. $3n + 5 = 350$. Subtract 5 from both sides and then divide by 3 to get 115.

27. **C** If you see something that can be multiplied, do it. $p(p - 3) = p^2 - 3p$, so $x = p^2 - 3p$. To find $x + 2$, we just add 2 to both sides to get $x + 2 = p^2 - 3p + 2$.

28. **D** Good vocab review, "product" means multiply. So $(3bm^4)(2b^4) = 6m^4b^5$. Notice that I did not add the exponents $4 + 4$ because m and b are different letters, and we add only when the letters are the same. Also, notice that the order of the variables does not matter; mb is the same as bm.

29. **C** If $b = 2$, then $a^{-3} = (2)^{-9}$ or $a^{-3} = \dfrac{1}{2^9} = 0.002$.

This is a "hard" question because most students get intimated by the negative exponents, and give up, but with our strategies, it's easy. Just "Use the Answers." Try each answer choice to find which one works. Choice C works since $(8)^{-3} = 0.002$.

30. **C** The graph shown represents $y = ax + b$, and we want an answer that shows $y = 3ax + b$. So we want a line that is 3 times steeper than the one in the question, and since b did not change, we want the same y intercept. So choice C is correct.

31. **12** Draw a blank for each option. Then write in the number of possibilities that can fill each option. There are 2 possibilities for slogan, 2 for shirt color, and 3 for size, so $\underline{2} \times \underline{2} \times \underline{3} = 12$.

32. **B** 0.7% equals 0.007. Each year the population of the colony will increase by a factor of 1.007, so $10{,}000(1.007)^t$.

33. **$\dfrac{1}{2}$ = 0.5** Probability $= \dfrac{\text{want}}{\text{total}}$, so the probability of selecting a prime number is $\dfrac{3}{6}$ which reduces to $\dfrac{1}{2}$ or 0.5. Remember, you need to reduce $\dfrac{3}{6}$ to get credit; the machine would not accept $\dfrac{3}{6}$ as the correct answer. Repeat after me, "Reducing is my friend . . . " or just use your calculator to get a decimal.

34. **B** Simply plug each answer in for the variable. If $m = 2$, then the three numbers in the list are 2, 5, 2. $m + 3$, which equals 5, is not the median. But when $m = 4$, the three numbers are 6, 7, 8. Thus, $m + 3$, which equals 7, is the middle number.

35. **A** We love these! Since m is positive, the U-shaped graph must open up and since n is zero, the y intercept must be zero. Choice A is the answer!

36. **3** The given equation is not in the standard form for a circle, $(x - h)^2 + (y - k)^2 = r^2$, so we need to complete the square to put it into standard form, as follows:
$x^2 + 4x + y^2 - 2y = 4$
$(x^2 + 4x + 4) - 4 + (y^2 - 2y + 1) - 1 = 4$
$(x + 2)^2 + (y - 1)^2 - 5 = 4$
$(x + 2)^2 + (y - 1)2 = 9$.

37. **D** Nice vocab review. Remember that "consecutive" means in a row, "odd" means numbers like 1, 3, 5, 7, 9, and "integer" means no decimals. So just choose 4 consecutive odd integers and divide each by 3 to see the remainder for each. Depending on the numbers you chose, the correct answer might be in a different order than your numbers.

38. **C** "Use the Answers." Try each answer choice in the equation.

 I. $|8 - 2| = 6$ correct
 II. $|-4 - 2| = |-6| = 6$ correct
 III. $|-3 - 2| = |-5| = 5 \neq 6$ incorrect

So I and II are correct and choice C is the answer.

39. **B** This is a sequence question. Continue the sequence until you have seven terms: 6, 10, 18, 34, 66, 130, **258**.

40. **C** $(i - 3)(i - 3) = i^2 - 6i + 9$. Since $i^2 = -1$, we have $-1 - 6i + 9 = 8 - 6i$.

41. **A** Plug $x = -2$ and simplify. $x(2s^2 - 2) = -2(2s^2 - 2) = -4x^2 + 4$. CARELESS ERROR BUSTER: Remember to distribute the negative sign!

42. **C** Plug 2 in for x and then FOIL $(y - 2)^2$. You can use the algebra trick for FOILing a binomial if you know it; and if you don't, no sweat, just do it out: $(y - 2)^2 = (y - 2)(y - 2) = y^2 - 2y - 2y + 4 = y^2 - 4y + 4$. CARELESS ERROR BUSTER: When you FOIL, remember the middle term!

43. **D** Point M is between -4 and -8 on the number line, so D is the only choice that works.

44. **D** This is a straightforward transformation. The parent function $g(x)$ needs to be shifted 1 unit down. If you memorize the transformations, this question is easy; a down transformation would be $y = g(x) - 1$. If you did not memorize the transformations, get to it, you silly slacker. Or, you could graph each choice on your calculator and see which one yields results that are all 1 unit down from the parent.

45. $\dfrac{\pi}{6}$ The angles of a triangle add up to 180°, so the third angle must be 30°. The question asks for the answer in radians, so convert degrees to radians, as follows:

$$(30)\dfrac{\pi}{180} = \dfrac{\pi}{6}.$$

CARELESS ERROR BUSTER: Make sure to finish the question.

46. **C** $\sec\theta$ is the reciprocal of $\cos\theta$, so we need $\cos\theta = \dfrac{1}{2}$, so $\theta = 60$.

47. **A** If y is inversely proportional to x^2, then $(y)(x^2) = k$, so when $y = \dfrac{1}{2}$ when $x = 2$, $(\dfrac{1}{2})(2^2) = 2 = k$, so for what is x when $y = \dfrac{1}{8}$, we plug in to get $(\dfrac{1}{8})(x^2) = 2$ and get $x = 4$.

48. **12** Taking the square root of a negative and dividing by zero are undefined. So, in this case, if $x = 25$, we have division by zero, and the function is undefined.

49. **D** There are 2 oranges to every 3 purple crayons, so there are 5 total, or actually some multiple of 5, so choice D is correct.

50. **D**

Glossary

30°, 60°, 90° triangle   a triangle with angles that measure 30°, 60°, 90° has sides that measure x, $2x$, and $x\sqrt{3}$. This is shown in the info box at the beginning of every SAT Math section.

45°, 45°, 90° triangle   an isosceles right triangle. Its sides have lengths x, x, and $x\sqrt{2}$. This is shown in the info box at the beginning of every SAT Math section.

absolute value $|-3|$ means "the absolute value of −3." "Absolute value" means after you do the math between the bars, ditch the negative sign!
- $|-3| = 3$
- $|3| = 3$
- $|-3 - 6| = |-9| = 9$

arithmetic mean   anytime the SAT prints the word "average," they follow it with "(arithmetic mean)." This is simply a clarification and a synonym for "average." They are just referring to the normal average that you are used to, so ignore "(arithmetic mean)."

average   The "average" of a list of numbers is found by adding them and dividing by how many there are.

$$\text{Average} = \frac{\text{sum}}{\text{number of items}}$$

The SAT also uses the sum formula:

Sum = (avg.) × (number of items)

bar graphs   graphs that compare the values of several items, such as sales of different toothpastes.

bisect   to cut into two equal parts. An angle bisector cuts an angle into two equal parts, and a segment bisector cuts a segment into two equal parts.

careless errors   these are bad, "mmmkay."

cartesian plane   a fancy term for the normal grid that you graph lines on.

consecutive even/odd numbers   even or odd numbers ordered in a row from lowest to highest such as 4, 6, 8, 10 or 3, 5, 7, 9.

consecutive numbers   numbers ordered in a row from lowest to highest such as 7, 8, 9, 10.

constant term   this term really throws some kids, but it just means a letter in place of a number, kinda like a variable, except that it won't vary.

cross-multiply   a method of solving proportions on the SAT. To solve for x in $\frac{5}{12} = \frac{x}{40}$, cross-multiply to get $(5)(40) = 12x$ and divide by 12 to get x alone.

different numbers   numbers that are . . . ummm . . . different.

directly proportional   also called "direct variation," means "x times some number gives y." The formula for this relationship is $y = kx$.

donut   the area of a donut equals the area of the larger circle minus the area of the donut hole.

drawn to scale   every diagram on the SAT is drawn to scale unless it states, "Note: Figure not drawn to scale." When a diagram is not drawn to scale, redraw it.

equiangular triangle   a triangle with all angles equal, which means that they each must equal 60°. The triangle is therefore also equilateral.

equilateral triangle   a triangle with all sides equal and all 60° angles.

even/odd   even numbers are 2, 4, 6, 8, . . . ; odd numbers are 1, 3, 5, 7, ...

exponents, laws of
- $n^6 \times n^2 = n^8$
- $\dfrac{n^6}{n^2} = n^4$
- $(n^6)^2 = n^{12}$
- $n^0 = 1$
- $n^1 = n$
- $n^{-2} = \dfrac{1}{n^2}$
- $2n^2 + n^2 = 3n^2$
- $2n + n^2$ does not combine
- $n^{\frac{4}{3}} = \sqrt[3]{n^4}$

exterior angle   an angle outside a triangle that equals the sum of the two nonadjacent interior angles.

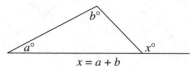

$x = a + b$

factors   numbers that divide into a number evenly (i.e., without a remainder).
Example: The factors of 48 are 1, 2, 3, 4, 6, 8, 12, 16, 24, 48.

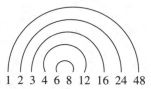

1 2 3 4 6 8 12 16 24 48

functions   the cause of much fear in teenagers. A type of equation, like $y = mx + b$. To show that an equation is a function, sometimes people replace the y with $f(x)$ or $g(x)$ or $h(x)$.

$f(x)$ is just a fancy way of saying y. So $f(x) = 2x - 1$ means the same as $y = 2x - 1$.

$f(3)$ means "plug 3 in for x" and $f(m) = 9$ means, "What did we plug into the equation for x to get a result of 9?"

info box   the box of math info and formulas provided at the beginning of every SAT Math section.

integer   a number without decimals or fractions, such as $-3, -2, -1, 0, 1, 2, 3, \ldots$ This is the single most common SAT Math vocab word!

inversely proportional   also called "inverse variation," means some number divided by x equals y. The formula is $y = \dfrac{k}{x}$.

isosceles triangle   a triangle with at least two congruent sides. The two angles opposite the two congruent sides are also congruent.

linear pair   two adjacent angles that form a line and add up to $180°$.

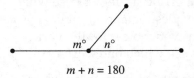

$m + n = 180$

line graph   display of how data changes, often over time.

"Make It Real."   the strategy to use when you see <u>variables</u> in the question and <u>variables</u> in the answer choices, especially for word problems. Choose real numbers in place of the variables, and the question becomes much easier.

math genius   somebody who has mastered all 50 Skills from *McGraw–Hill's Top 50 Skills for a Top Score: SAT Math*.

median   the middle term in a list of numbers. For the list 2, 5, 7, 8, 8, the number 7 is the median.

mode   the most frequent term in a list of numbers. For the list 2, 5, 7, 8, 8, the number 8 is the mode.

multiples   all the numbers that are divisible by a certain number.

The multiples of 3 are 3, 6, 9, 12, 15, 18, 21, etc.

multiple-choice questions   questions that offer answer choices:

Ⓐ

Ⓑ

Ⓒ

Ⓓ

order of difficulty   questions in SAT Math sections are arranged from easiest to hardest.

ordered pair   a fancy term for a pair of coordinates (x, y) on the xy coordinate plane.

parallel lines   lines in a plane that never intersect and have equal slopes, like $\dfrac{2}{3}$ and $\dfrac{2}{3}$.

perpendicular lines   lines that intersect at a right (90°) angle and have negative reciprocal slopes, like $\dfrac{2}{3}$ and $-\dfrac{3}{2}$.

pictographs   graphs that use small pictures to represent data. The key to pictographs lies in noticing the legend. If each icon represents 8 books, then 1/2 of an icon represents 4 books, not 1/2 of a book.

pie graph   a technique to represent information as part of a pie.

positive/negative numbers   positive numbers are greater than 0 and negative numbers are less than 0.

prime factors   the factors of a number that are also prime numbers. The prime factors of 48 are 2 and 3. These are the factors of 48 that also happen to be prime numbers.

prime number   a number whose only factors are 1 and itself, such

as 2, 3, 5, 7, 11, 13, 17, 19, . . . The number 1 is NOT considered prime, and the number 2 is the only even prime number.

probability   a measure of the likelihood of something happening. To determine probability on the SAT, use the equation Probability $= \dfrac{\text{want}}{\text{total}}$.

proportion   two ratios set equal to each other, for example, $\dfrac{5}{12} = \dfrac{10}{24}$ or $\dfrac{5}{12} = \dfrac{x}{40}$. To solve a proportion, cross-multiply.

Pythagorean theorem   when given two sides of a right triangle, we can find the third with the formula $a^2 + b^2 = c^2$.

quadratic equation   an equation with a variable such as x that is squared. For example, $y = ax^2 + bx + c$. In such an equation, the a tells whether the U-shaped graph opens up or down, and c is the y intercept.

ratio   a relationship between two numbers, such as 7 cups of oats to 2 cups of sugar. It can be written as $7 : 2$ or $\dfrac{7}{2}$ or even 7 to 2. The SAT likes to see if you can play with ratios. For example, 4 boys to 5 girls could also be expressed 5 girls to 9 students.

real number   any number except for i, such as $-3, -2.2, 0, \sqrt{2}, \pi$.

reflection   a mirror image. In the diagram below, line m is the reflection of line l over the x-axis. Reflected lines over the x-axis or y-axis have negative slopes, like $\dfrac{2}{3}$ and $-\dfrac{2}{3}$.

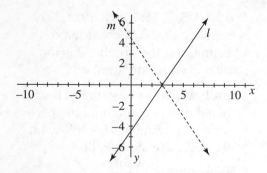

remainders   what's left over when you use long division.

$$
\begin{array}{r}
52\ \text{r}1 \\
7\,\overline{)\,365} \\
\underline{-35} \\
15 \\
\underline{-14} \\
1
\end{array}
$$

right triangle   a triangle with a right (90°) angle. When you see a right triangle, use $a^2 + b^2 = c^2$ to find the length of a missing side.

scatterplots   graphs that compare two aspects of a group. When the SAT gives a scatterplot, it often asks you to name the equation of the line that best fits the data. Just sketch a line, estimate its y intercept and slope, and choose the equation (see Skill 30) that matches best.

similar triangles   triangles that have congruent corresponding angles and proportional sides; one is a shrinky version of the other.

slope   the measure of a line's steepness; the steeper the line, the bigger the slope. In the equations $y = mx + b$ or $y = ax + b$, m or a is the slope, and b is the y intercept.

$$
\text{Slope} = \frac{y_1 - y_2}{x_1 - x_2}
$$

special right triangles   a 30°, 60°, 90° triangle with sides x, $2x$, and $x\sqrt{3}$, or a 45°, 45°, 90° triangle with sides x, x, and $x\sqrt{2}$. These are shown in the info box at the beginning of every SAT Math section.

springboard strategy   on the SAT, when something can be factored, FOILed, reduced, or simplified, . . . do it.

student-produced response questions   SAT Math questions that are not followed by answer choices.

tables   charts that display information in rows and columns. Usually the SAT asks you to use the last row or column, which shows totals.

transformation   a change that happens when we add, subtract, multiply, or divide a number into an equation that causes the graph to move up, down, left, or right. It might even make it skinnier or fatter.

translation   conversion of word problems from English to math.

transversal   a line that crosses two parallel lines, forming 8 angles.

triangle   a closed shape formed by three sides. The angles in a triangle add up to 180°.

units digit   a fancy term for the "ones" digit in a number, like the 2 in 672.

"Use the Answers"   a terrific strategy to use when you see variables in the question and numbers in the answers. Try the answer choices for the variables in the question to see which one works.

"Use the Diagram"   a great strategy that says since diagrams on the SAT are drawn accurately, we can use the diagrams to estimate the answer to many questions. When the answer choices contain a square root ($\sqrt{\ }$) or the symbol pi (π), always translate to decimals.

vertical angles   two angles whose sides form two pairs of opposite rays. Vertical angles are congruent.

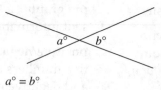

$a° = b°$

"what is m in terms of p and q"   means solve for m or use algebra to get m alone.

xy coordinate plane   a fancy term for the normal xy grid that your graph lines on.